Arnis Self-Defense

Arnis Self-Defense

Stick, Blade, and Empty-Hand Combat
Techniques of the Philippines

José G. Paman

BLUE SNAKE BOOKS

Berkeley, California

Published by Blue Snake Books / Frog, Ltd.

Blue Snake Books / Frog, Ltd. books
are distributed by North Atlantic Books
P.O. Box 12327
Berkeley, California 94712

Cover photograph of the author
courtesy of Alex G. Paman
Cover and book design by Brad Greene
Printed in the United States of America

Blue Snake Books' publications are available through most bookstores. For further information, call 800-337-2665 or visit our website at www.northatlanticbooks.com or www.bluesnakebooks.com.

Substantial discounts on bulk quantities are available to corporations, professional associations, and other organizations. For details and discount information, contact our special sales department.

PLEASE NOTE: The creators and publishers of this book disclaim any liabilities for loss in connection with following any of the practices, exercises, and advice contained herein. To reduce the chance of injury or any other harm, the reader should consult a professional before undertaking this or any other martial arts, movement, meditative arts, health, or exercise program. The instructions and advice printed in this book are not in any way intended as a substitute for medical, mental, or emotional counseling with a licensed physician or healthcare provider.

Library of Congress Cataloging-in-Publication Data

Paman, José G.
    Arnis self-defense : stick, blade, and empty hand combat techniques of the Philippines / by José G. Paman.
        p. cm.
    Includes bibliographical references.
    ISBN-13: 978-1-58394-177-5 (trade paper)
    ISBN-10: 1-58394-177-0 (trade paper)
  1. Escrima. 2. Martial arts—Philippines. I. Title.
    GV1114.38.P36 2007
    796.815—dc22
                                        2006035427
                                            CIP
        1 2 3 4 5 6 7 8 9 UNITED 12 11 10 09 08 07

Dedication

This volume is lovingly dedicated to my sons Joey and Nico, who have given me purpose and direction; to arnis practitioners around the world for carrying on the centuries-old traditions of the fighting arts of the Philippines; and to my fallen comrade-at-arms Lt. Ray Anthony Samonte Alfabeto (AFP), who paid the ultimate price in the Philippine jungle while fighting the insurgency.

Acknowledgments

Sincere thanks to the Sacramento Pamans for their unfailing support; to Grandmaster Ernesto Amador Presas Sr. for being my mentor in Kombatan arnis and Shotokan karate; to Grandmasters Roberto Presas and Pepe Yap and to my early Arjuken training partners Rey de la Merced, Ricardo Rivera, Alex Pangilinan, and Julian Valdoria for their tremendous contributions to my early martial arts development; to my other instructors, Dee Se Giok and Co Chi Po (Ngo Cho kung fu), Rod Goodwin (goshin jitsu), and Don Cross (danzan-ryu jujitsu) for the vital lessons; to Jess O'Brien for the referral; and to my first black belt student, Doug Hudson, for his able assistance during the preparation of this volume. Special appreciation is also extended my father, Prof. José A. Paman, for proofreading the first draft and offering vital corrections.

Important Note

The information and techniques described in this book can be dangerous and may result in serious injury if not practiced with caution and the proper supervision of an expert. The author, publisher, and distributors disclaim any liability for all injuries to person or property that may occur from the use of said information. It is the responsibility of the reader to comply with all federal, state, and local laws pertaining to the use of impact, edged, and flexible weapons.

Table of Contents

Preface

It was the summer of 1971. Like most Manila youths, I had caught the martial arts bug from watching films that featured such masters as Philippine karate champion Tony Ferrer and the Gonzales siblings Roberto, Rolando, and Magna (the offspring of Okinawan Shorin-ryu master Latino Gonzales). Kung fu movies from Hong Kong had also started to flood the Manila movie houses.

Arnis, which had been a rather obscure martial art up until that point, began to appear on TV programs and in demonstrations given in local parks. The Arjuken Karate Association stood on the corner of Quezon Boulevard and Claro M. Recto Avenue in the heart of Quiapo, Manila's bustling business district. I had been to this gym before to watch classes, but that summer, my fascination got the best of me and I decided to join up. The training program, headed by a young Ernesto A. Presas, offered classes in karate, arnis, jujitsu, kendo, and Okinawan weaponry. I signed up and began a lifelong study of arnis.

Introduction

The art of arnis was developed over several centuries under actual battle conditions. It is a pragmatic, sensible, and versatile self-defense system. Its lessons will help you deal with all levels of conflict ranging from minor annoyances to life-threatening predicaments. By practicing the simple and effective skills of this Filipino martial art, you will learn a powerful method of self-preservation—a very useful tool for today's volatile and unpredictable world.

The creation of arnis cannot be attributed to a single individual or even a group of individuals. It is the product of Filipino resourcefulness and creativity, and it is distinct from the martial arts of any other nation. Arnis prominently emphasizes the qualities of simplicity, directness, and practicality.

Arnis is straightforward and easy to learn, and its basic techniques are identified using a simple numbering system. Arnis utilizes a small number of core techniques to address endless possibilities; the basic lines of attack, introduced early in training, cover all of the different angles from which an assailant's attack might come. Unlike in many other martial arts, there are generally no elaborate rituals associated with its practice.

Arnis is meant for combat, not show. The practitioner's sole aim is survival, and his or her goal is to neutralize the enemy immediately. Therefore, arnis does not use flashy techniques; there is no distinction between form and application. Arnis tries to anticipate the natural progression of a fight as it spans different distances (requiring short-, medium-, and long-range fighting skills) and employs different weapons. Training emphasizes flexible responses rather than rigid, prearranged actions. A student quickly gains the ability to effectively deal with any number of attack scenarios.

Arnis is realistic. A fundamental truth of combat is one should not face an attacker bare-handed if he has the opportunity to arm himself. In recognition of this, arnis emphasizes weapons training first. The arnis arsenal also reflects the pragmatic quality of the art: the stick, knife, and *bolo* (machete) have the most value in modern combat. It is fairly useless to be proficient at the three-section staff, the broadsword, or the spear if you are unable to carry these weapons with you at all times. In addition, arnis techniques can easily be executed using improvised weapons. The art does not, however, ignore empty-hand techniques, as you might find yourself in a predicament where a weapon is not readily available or you might drop your weapon in the course of combat.

Arnis is adaptable and versatile. The art developed during Spanish colonial times and absorbed European fencing theories and methods. (This is evident in existing arnis terminology; Spanish words such as *espada, baston,* and *daga* are used to describe its weapons and techniques.) Some practices found in European swordplay were also incorporated into arnis, such as the use of a numbering system as a tool to teach basic cutting strokes and angles and the tradition of using a short weapon like the dagger to complement a longer weapon like the sword or the long stick.

Arnis continues to develop. It is an open-ended system that allows for individual expression within the general framework of its fundamental principles. Effective methods of combat, whatever their origins, have been adopted into its repertoire, and continue to be added. The native grappling art of *buno* (*dumog* to people from the Visayas region), for instance, was added as a bare-handed complement to the stick and blade arts. Western-style boxing and wrestling were likewise incorporated, as were elements of jujitsu and judo (especially during World War II and immediately afterward). Techniques from karate, kung fu, and aikido have also found their way into arnis' arsenal.

With little or no modification, arnis can be used for civilian self-defense, military combat, or law-enforcement purposes. For civilians, arnis offers a means of protection to be used solely for self-defense. For the military, its skills are readily applicable to eliminating sentries and mastering close-quarter combat in areas like jungles, caves, tunnels, and barracks. For law-enforcement purposes, arnis is effective for disarming and apprehending suspects or for riot control. The basic angles and maneuvers taught allow students to use and to defend against any type of weapon or attack. Arnis is constantly evolving, adapting to changing combat requirements.

Last but not least, unlike other Asian martial arts, arnis does not encourage pacifist tendencies. In general, arnis teachers are not known for being overtly philosophical or for placing many restraints on their students. Prominently absent in arnis training is the directive to refrain from actually using one's skills in combat (though most teachers do stress that students should only use their skills for legitimate self-defense purposes). When faced with a valid reason to employ his or her combative skills, the arnis exponent applies whatever measure is necessary to neutralize the threat. Indeed, a major element of the spirit of arnis is the fact that the people who created the art have been involved in one form of conflict or another for centuries.

Arnis skills were born of battle and the need for survival, and they continue to be transmitted plainly, directly, and without ceremony from one generation to the next.

Part One

The Story of Arnis

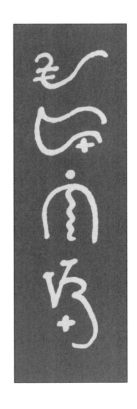

Chapter 1

The Name

Combat is as old as humankind. Whether people needed to defend themselves against predatory beasts or against other human beings, they used any implements at their disposal, and even their bare hands, to do so. Over time, these basic survival actions developed into organized training systems. Influenced by geography, political climate, existing conflicts and threats, cultural and religious preferences, and other factors, people in every country have forged unique self-defense methods. In the Philippines, these systems are called by a number of names—*eskrima, garote, estokada, fraile, baston*—but the most widely accepted title is *arnis* (ar-NEES), an all-encompassing term for the Filipino martial arts. All of these systems are based on a singular method of combat training that initially teaches stick-fighting skills and then progresses to blade and empty-hand techniques.

The existence of so many different titles for what is essentially the same art reflects how much Filipino martial artists emphasized the practical in the early days of arnis' development and practice. In older times, Filipinos were more focused on developing effective combat skills than preserving a standard title for these skills for later reference. For some fighting methods or training systems, a particular term may never have been designated. Therefore, each new generation of Filipino martial artists used different terms when naming the methods they taught.

Arnis is the most common and most recognized name for the Filipino martial arts in the Philippines, especially in Manila, where a major revival of the native arts occurred in the 1960s. It is a derivation and abbreviation of the Spanish term *arnes de mano* or "harness of the hand," which was a reference to the costumes of the *Moro-Moro* performers of Spanish colonial times. (*Moro-Moro* is a socioreligious play wherein performers reenact the triumph of the Christian Spaniards over the Muslim Moors at Granada.) The Filipino poet Francisco Balagtas (also known as Francisco Baltazar) made reference to the term arnis in his epic 1853 poem "Florante at Laura"; in it he described the protagonists' skills in arnis and *buno* (native wrestling). The first book written on the Filipino martial arts also used the word arnis. Written in Tagalog by Placido Yambao and released in 1957, *Mga Karunungan sa Larong Arnis (Skills in Arnis Play)* provided the first attempt at documenting arnis' history and techniques.

Certain other names are still commonly used, albeit on a regional basis. Eskrima comes from the Spanish *esgrima* (swordplay), and it's the second most commonly used term in the Philippines (it's widely used in Cebu, and on other islands in the central Visayas region). The Doce Pares Association, one of the oldest native martial arts organizations in the Philippines, refers to its combat system as eskrima, as did the arnis pioneer and master Angel Cabales, who was the first instructor to open a commercial Filipino martial arts school in the United States.

Garote, another common name, was derived from *garrote* (heavy stick or cudgel). Estokada refers to the sword known as *estoque* (*estoc* in French), which is also used in bullfighting. Fraile, curiously, is the Spanish word for friar; fencing was reportedly a common activity among the Spanish friars of colonial times. Far from the peaceful modern-day clergy, the warrior priests of that era were driven by necessity to learn combat skills to help defend themselves and Christian Filipinos against attacks by

Islamic pirates. Finally, baston is also used—it means "cane," which is a main weapon in the Filipino martial arts arsenal.

It is important to also take a look at the name *kali,* which is commonly used by American practitioners of arnis. Placido Yambao's book *Mga Karunungan sa Larong Arnis* mentioned the word kali as a designation for the ancient Filipino martial arts. That book, in turn, was listed in the bibliography of Donn Draeger and Robert W. Smith's seminal volume *Asian Fighting Arts* (later re-released as *Comprehensive Asian Fighting Arts*). The latter book appears to have been the main source for the history chapters of many subsequent works on arnis; it's likely that this is why a few present-day martial artists use the name kali to describe their arts.

By choosing the name kali, creative martial arts instructors and writers have attached a Moro motif to their styles in order to generate mystique and give the impression that they somehow have a connection to the fierce fighters of the Mindanao and Sulu regions of the southern Philippines. (Moro was a term first used by the Spanish to describe the natives of the Islamic south.) Historically, Moros were regarded as unstoppable in battle—the term "leatherneck" arose during the U.S. occupation of the islands in the late 1800s when marines were forced to wear thick neck protectors to defend against decapitation by these warriors. It is said that the .45-caliber pistol was developed during this time because the standard .38-caliber pistol could not stop a determined Moro fighter. Accounts exist of blade-wielding Moros being riddled by .38-caliber bullets or run through by American bayonets, only to continue their attack. Some soldiers observed the Moros pulling the bayonets deeper into their bodies to bridge the gap between them and their American adversaries and reach them with their own blades. Possessed of an intense warrior mindset, many Moros would not stop until they were dead. There is, however, no verifiable evidence linking arnis to the Islamic combat styles of *silat* and *kuntao,* which were practiced in relative secrecy in the south. (Both sides have been in fierce and bloody conflict for decades.)

In fact, kali was unheard of in the Philippines until after the emergence of the book *Filipino Martial Arts* (compiled by Dan Inosanto, Gilbert L. Johnson, and George Foon), which was released in 1980. With the distribution of that book, the term kali gradually gained some popularity in the United States, as the "mother art" of purportedly Islamic origin that gave rise to the other Filipino martial arts systems.

Until the late 1980s, if you asked a native Filipino martial arts master or practitioner about kali, he would likely have made reference to the Ray Harryhausen animated movie *The Golden Voyage of Sinbad,* which was a major hit in the Philippines. The term simply does not appear in Filipino oral or written history, linguistics, mythology, or folklore. Respected Filipino researchers, such as Felipe P. Jocano, Jr., Dr. Ned Nepangue, and Celestino Macachor, have written at length about the term's lack of validity. That it is even recognized in the Philippines is thanks to the influx of books and videos produced by Americans, as well as the influx of practitioners from the United States seeking instruction in "kali." When approached by American students who sought to learn kali, native masters simply taught them arnis and called it kali. So, although it may serve as an alternative, modern designation for the Filipino martial arts, the term kali does not have the purported Islamic historical connection commonly attributed to it by Western practitioners of arnis.

Chapter 2

Through the Mists of Time

Arnis Timeline

Early: 1500s to 1920—Scattered references to arnis are recorded by European chroniclers, and native accounts are passed on by word of mouth.

Middle: 1920 to 1970—The Labangon Fencing Club is founded in Cebu; many other arnis clubs follow.

Modern: 1970 to Present—Manila's Martial Arts Golden Age. Contemporary trends in arnis emerge.

Known in Asia as the Pearl of the Orient, the Philippines is made up of 7,107 islands and is populated by various tribal groups speaking over 70 dialects and sub-dialects. Located in a strategic sector of the Asian continent, it represents a vital geographic gateway to the region.

Scientific evidence indicates that modern-day Filipinos are descended from several groups of inhabitants who arrived at the islands at different times. The original natives were alternately known as the Ita, Agta, Baluga, and Negrito (a Spanish term) people. These primitive people had a culture belonging to the Paleolithic Age; some 30,000 years ago,

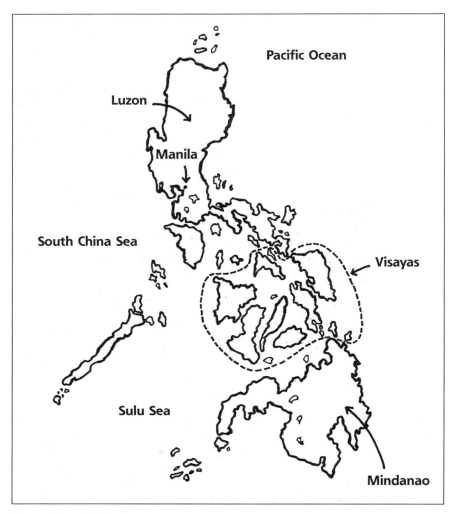

Map of the Philippines.

they walked over land bridges that connected the Philippines to the Asian mainland. Current descendants of the Itas live in areas of Zambales and Pampanga provinces in the northern Philippines.

Following the submergence of the land bridges, another Asian group migrated to the islands. The seafaring Indonesians came in two waves, the first arrival happened in around 3000 BC and the second in around 1000 BC. The Indonesian culture was more advanced than that of the Itas. They farmed, weaved clothing, and possessed hunting and fishing skills.

Finally, the Malays navigated their way to the islands. Their migration consisted of three waves. The first came around 200 BC, when a group of headhunting people who were the ancestors of the present-day Ilongots, Bontoks, and Kalingas of Northern Luzon arrived. The second wave arrived around 100 AD and was made up of the alphabet-using Malays, who were the ancestors of the modern-day Tagalogs, Visayans, Ilokanos, Bikolanos, Pampangos, and other Christianized tribes. The last wave was the Muslim Malays, who arrived in the fourteenth century and introduced Islamic culture and religion to the Philippines. The descendants of this group now inhabit the southern provinces of the country.

When they arrived, the Malays were the most advanced people to come to the Philippines. They not only practiced agriculture and weaved clothing, but also made pottery and manufactured metal tools and weapons. They utilized weaponry, including swords, daggers (called *daga* or *patalim*, both signifying short, edged weapons), spears *(sibat)*, bows and arrows *(pana at palaso)*, blowguns *(sumpit)*, and shields *(kalasag)*. Some of these weapons are still taught in modern-day arnis.

The early Filipinos had customs, traditions, and ways of life quite unlike those of the surrounding Asian peoples. The basic community unit was called a *barangay* and included up to 100 families. A chieftain, called a *datu*, ruled over the *barangay*. Members of the community belonged to one of three social classes: the *maharlika* (the nobles), the *timagua* (the free men), or the *alipin* (the slave class).

Early Filipinos used a system of writing known as the *baybayin* (or *alibata*), which resembled an ancient writing style of India. The *baybayin* was composed of three vowels (a; e or i, which were used interchange-

An example of *baybayin*, the ancient Philippine system of writing, is illustrated here in a passage from the *Doctrina Cristiana*, the first book published in the Philippines. The book included Catholic prayers rendered in Spanish and in Tagalog, the latter of which was written in both the Latin alphabet and *baybayin* script.

ably; and o or u, which were used interchangeably) and fourteen consonants. Diacritical marks were used to indicate variations of pronunciation. Few examples of this script exist today, but the *Doctrina Cristiana* (1593), the first book published in the Philippines, depicted the writing as traveling from left to right. Double vertical lines divided the sentences.

Antonio Pigafetta, who served as a chronicler for Spain, recorded that on March 16, 1521, Ferdinand Magellan landed on the island of Homonhon. A native of Portugal who sailed under the Spanish flag, Magellan offered to find for the king of Spain a route to the east by sailing westward. Magellan endured a hard voyage, and he dubbed the Philippines the Archipielago de San Lazaro, (after the Catholic saint Lazarus, who was resurrected by Christ), because landing there saved him and his crew from imminent death.

With the aid of the Spanish priests in his group, Magellan immediately began the process of converting the natives he encountered to the Catholic faith. Some welcomed these foreigners, who brought gifts of mirrors, combs, bells, and ivory along with their religion. One chieftain, however, violently expressed his disapproval. The fiery Lapu Lapu organized his warriors and attacked Magellan's crew on April 27, 1521, just over one month after they had landed on Philippine shores. Magellan and several of his men were killed in the ensuing battle, felled by the bladed weapons and fire-hardened sticks of the natives—an example of the early use of weaponry. The ships *Concepción, Trinidad,* and *Victoria* sailed away without their leader.

In 1565 another Spanish conquistador named Miguel Lopez de Legaspi successfully established a fort in Cebu and renamed the country Las Yslas Filipinas, after King Philip II of Spain. Six years later, most of the Philippines was under the control of a central Spanish government. Total domination by the Spanish over the native Filipinos continued for over 300 years. They enforced adherence to the Catholic religion, insisting that this would civilize the conquered "savages," whom they referred to as *indios,* a derogatory term that denoted stupidity. It's not surprising that the first book to be published in the Philippines was the *Doctrina Cristiana,* a collection of prayers. The Spanish also changed the names of their subjects, as they found it difficult to pronounce and remember native names. In 1849, under the Decree of Cognomen (cognomen is a Latin term that means "familiar name" or "recognized name"), they brought in two directories from Spain and forced Filipinos to adopt a Spanish name. Although the majority would comply, some resisted this imposition.

Unlike the strategies they used in both Central America and South America, the Spaniards took a different approach to conquering the

Philippines. Cognizant of the different dialects spoken among the various tribes, they purposely refrained from teaching the Spanish language to the general public. This was a calculated effort to prevent the disparate tribes from speaking a common tongue and thereby being able to band together in revolt. In later years, only the elite among native Filipinos would learn Spanish.

"Divide and conquer" is an effective basic principle of warfare. Dividing an enemy force into smaller, more-manageable components makes it much easier to defeat. This tactic was not necessary in the Philippines, as the natives were already quite divided by tribal languages, regionalism, and long-standing conflicts and hostilities; the Spaniards only had to make sure that the tribes stayed that way. In this respect, the Filipinos did not lose their native dialects under foreign rule. (There is nonetheless a substantial Spanish influence present in the contemporary Philippine language—some 2,000 Spanish words have been borrowed in direct or corrupted forms.)

Although they failed to unite under a common tongue, Filipinos were connected to each other by their fierce yearning for freedom from foreign rule and by an equally fierce method of combat that would come to be known as arnis.

Way of the Jungle Warrior

The paucity of reliable records makes it extremely difficult to determine the origin of arnis. As mentioned earlier, records indicate that the Malays, who came to the islands starting in 200 BC, used a variety of weapons, some of which are still used in contemporary arnis practice. Which maneuvers they executed to use these weapons, however, remains unknown. There is evidence that Lapu Lapu and his forces used both club-type and bladed weapons when they disposed of Magellan and drove his ships from the islands. Whether they used actual arnis techniques as they exist today, however, is still the subject of speculation.

Current martial arts researchers often mention that Spanish authorities banned the practice of arnis in 1764. An often-cited explanation for this prohibition is that the natives reputedly enjoyed arnis so much they began to neglect their crops, which were necessary for the survival of both the conquerors and the conquered. Simple logic would infer, however, that a practical people would never forsake such a basic need in favor of a pastime, however enjoyable that pastime may be. It is more likely that the Spanish banned the practice of arnis after witnessing the participants suffer injuries from the activity. Moreover, it is possible that skilled natives used arnis methods in encounters with the Spanish, and having seen its effectiveness, the Spanish reacted by prohibiting its practice. Regardless of whether or not any of these suppositions are factual, they still do not explain where arnis originated.

What is known is that arnis movements existed and were incorporated into native dance and stage plays like the *Moro-Moro,* the socioreligious play organized by the Spaniards that reenacted the triumph of the Christian Spanish over the Muslim Moors at Granada. In this play, Filipinos were made to dress up as princes, princesses, warriors, and laymen on both sides of the conflict. Simulated swordplay with live blades was included. The *Moro-Moro* phenomenon exists to this day as part of the Spanish legacy in the Philippines.

More recently, enterprising martial arts writers have concocted differing scenarios for the creation of arnis. Some versions border on the fantastic, including fanciful accounts of mythical figures like blind hermits, mysterious Islamic princesses, and Shaolin temple-like tunnels of death. Some accounts may be more credible than others, but due to the shortage of verifiable information, it is virtually impossible to ascertain where arnis actually originated. One thing is certain: arnis cannot be confined to dusty museums or exclusive libraries inaccessible to the common people; it resides permanently in the blood of the Filipino people.

Chapter 3

Portrait of a People

Any martial art is a reflection of the people who created it; likewise, the characteristics of the Filipino people have influenced the formation of arnis.

The Languages

The country has two official languages: Filipino, which is largely based on the Tagalog dialect (the name was drawn from *taga ilog* or "people of the river"), and English, which is the language of instruction in schools. Filipino is the language spoken by the common man and the means by which people of different tribes and regions communicate with one another. Speaking English allows Filipinos to readily communicate on a wider basis because of the universal nature of the language. The Philippines also has a tradition of literature in the Spanish language, a remnant of the long colonial period. Seven other major regional dialects are spoken in the country, namely Cebuano, Ilokano, Ilonggo, Bikolano, Waray-Waray, Pampango, and Pangasinense (also called Pangasinan and Pangalatok). The languages of Kinaray-a, Maranao, Maguindanao, and Tausug have also been added to this list.

Before the inauguration of the Philippine Commonwealth, English and Spanish were the official languages in the Philippines—there was no national language. In 1936 Philippine Commonwealth Act No. 184 directed the Institute of National Language to conduct a study of local dialects in order to establish a national language. The study recommended the adoption of Tagalog as the basis for what came to be known as Filipino. Tagalog is the native tongue of Metropolitan Manila and the southern Tagalog-region provinces of Bataan, Batangas, Bulacan, Cavite, Laguna, Mindoro, Nueva Ecija, Rizal, and Quezon. With the implementation of this recommendation, the term Filipino (Pilipino in the native tongue—the letter 'F' does not exist in the *abakada* alphabet) came to mean either the nationality or the national language of the people of the Philippines. The national language was reconfirmed under the Philippine Constitution drafted in 1987.

In the 1960s the so-called English Campaign was enforced upon grade-school students in some private schools in Manila. Students were forbidden to speak in Filipino; apparently, this was done to ensure their ability to communicate and compete in the international marketplace. Small fines were levied upon violators. Later, a hybrid variation known as Taglish (from TAGalog and EngLISH) emerged, in which Filipino and English words were mixed together freely in conversation. Taglish continues to be spoken in Manila and in many other Filipino communities both in the Philippines and overseas.

As noted earlier, some 2,000 Spanish words have been adopted into the current Filipino language. Some of these words are direct adaptations, while others represent corruptions of the original Spanish terms. Below are a few examples. Filipino terms are rendered based on the twenty-letter native *abakada* system of writing used today.

Filipino	Spanish	English
berdugo	verdugo	executioner
bintana	ventana	window
doble	doble	double
ekis	equis	the letter x
ispada	espada	sword
kadena	cadena	chain
krus	cruz	cross
kumusta	¿como esta?	salutation ("How are you doing?")
kutsilyo	cuchillo	knife
Moro	Moro	moor
pader	pared	wall
sundalo	soldado	soldier
tenedor	tenedor	fork

In addition to counting in their native language, most Filipinos can count in English and Spanish. If you observe arnis training in the Philippines, you'll hear instructors and practitioners counting in Filipino, English, and Spanish.

The Filipino writing system is based on that of the Latin alphabet and not—as in most Asian countries—on ideograms borrowed from the Chinese. The aforementioned *baybayin* fell into disuse long ago.

Interesting Note: Many arnis techniques and weapons are named after animals or everyday household items. The *binakoko* blade, for instance, derived its name from the *bakoko* fish. The *dinahong palay* blade was named after the *dahong palay,* a poisonous snake. Adding the letters "in" to the middle of some Filipino words creates another word meaning "to emulate." Thus, *payong* (umbrella) becomes *pinayong,* which means "umbrella-like movement." *Sawali,* a kind of native matting,

The Filipino Flag. The eight rays of the sun represent the first eight provinces to revolt against Spanish rule. The three stars located at each corner of the triangle symbolize the three main island groups of Luzon, Visayas, and Mindanao. The blue stripe stands for peace, the red stripe for bravery, and the white triangle for equality. The blue stripe is uppermost in times of peace and the reverse is observed, with the red stripe on top, in wartime.

becomes *sinawali,* a double stick method that uses a weaving pattern. *Puti,* the color white, becomes *pinuti,* a type of long blade.

Religion & Spiritual Beliefs

Unlike in the rest of Asia where variations of Buddhism, Hinduism, and Islam are prevalent, in the Philippines, ninety-five percent of the population practices the Christian religion; eighty-three percent are Roman Catholic. The Moro tribes of Mindanao and Sulu in the south, which follow Islam, represent a two-percent minority in the country.

Early Filipinos also believed in a supreme being, known as *bathala* to the Tagalog tribes. In addition, they believed in lesser gods and spirits, each of which having a distinct power or function.

Filipinos are known for their unique spiritual beliefs. Many, particularly those living in the rural areas, subscribe to a number of seemingly anachronistic concepts like the power of *agimat* or *anting anting* (amulets) and the practice of *hilot,* which is a holistic bodywork system said to be a special gift bestowed upon people of breech birth. *Hilot* is accompanied by *bulong,* which literally means "whisper," and signifies secret words that enable the healing effects of the massage. Many Filipinos also believe in a number of supernatural monsters *(aswang),* a cast of characters that includes the *kapre,* a tobacco-smoking, dark-skinned giant; the *tikbalang,* which has a horse's head and lower body and a man's torso and can turn victims into its kind by tricking them into eating a magic bread; the *tiyanak,* a baby demon that lures its victim to it by taking the form of a human infant and then bites the victim in the neck when he or she picks it up; and the *manananggal,* a demon that by day appears to be normal but by night grows wings and flies around killing unsuspecting victims and eating their internal organs.

Cultural and Social Characteristics

Filipinos express tremendous respect for family and for their elders in particular. Each household has a strict hierarchy; protocol is based on this system and strictly adhered to. Younger people are expected to remain silent as older people speak, and await permission to speak. They use the words *po* or *ho*—polite words that are inserted mid-sentence to signify respect for elders—when addressing parents, aunts, uncles, grandparents, and other older people. Elders are greeted with the phrase, "*mano po,*" which literally means, "Hand, please." As they say this phrase, the child or grandchild presses his or her forehead against the back of the elder's extended hand. (This custom, curiously, comes from Spanish colonial times and was said to have come about because the friars considered their subjects too dirty to be allowed to kiss their hands. The subjects' foreheads were then used to signify an acknowledgment of subjugation.) The oldest brother in a family is referred to as *kuya,* the second-oldest brother as *diko,* and the third one as *sangko.* Sisters are addressed as *ate, ditse,* and *sanse* respectively.

Filipinos are known for being extremely social in nature and enjoying any reason to join in celebration. In the tradition *bayanihan,* citizens of rural communities literally move entire houses from one location to another. During numerous *pistahan* (fiestas) held in provinces throughout the year—and often in honor of Catholic patron saints—homeowners frequently open their doors to anyone who wishes to stop in for a bite to eat or a drink. Standard fare, such as *lumpia* (eggrolls), *pansit* (noodles), *inihaw na baboy* (barbecued pork), *dinuguan* (blood stew), and *litson* (roast pig), as well as regional specialties, are served during these celebrations.

Even wakes for the deceased, known as *pulaw* or *lamay,* are observed in a unique way. Community members stay up all night to keep the deceased company, playing cards or mah jong, eating bread, and drinking coffee. An open microphone is often available, and the more daring mourners can belt out their favorite tunes to the accompaniment of an acoustic guitar or karaoke machine.

Paradoxically, Filipinos are also known for being warlike. Noted for their extreme hospitality toward friends, they typically exhibit polite manners and a love for peace and law-and-order—until a line is crossed. Although they are generally easygoing people always ready with a smile, Filipinos are also sensitive and can be dangerous if offended. "Best friend, worst enemy" is a common description attributed to them.

The Philippines has historically been an armed society. Based on their experiences with warfare against both foreign invaders and domestic enemies over the centuries, Filipinos have always appreciated the value of weapons. They have collectively experienced some form of combat from the 1500s onward and have fought against Spanish, American, and Japanese forces; domestic adversaries like the Hukbalahap (short for Hukbo ng Bayan Laban sa Hapon; Nation's Army Against the Japanese), the Communist insurgency, and the Islamic separatist movement; and coup attempts by seditious elements of the military. A popular saying is: Filipinos are so fond of conflict that when they ran out of foreign enemies, they turned on one another "katuwaan lang" or "just for kicks."

The worldwide phenomenon referred to as People Power is said to have originated in the Philippines in February 1986. Known within the Philippines as the EDSA Revolution (after Epifanio de los Santos Avenue, where the movement came to a dramatic conclusion), this historic episode united the urban citizenry, the powerful Roman Catholic church, the business elite, *and* the military against Ferdinand Marcos. On February 25, 1986, Marcos was deposed as a result, and Corazon Aquino, wife of slain Marcos rival Benigno Aquino, was installed in his place. Many Filipinos proudly claim that this event ultimately inspired citizens of other countries to topple many oppressive regimes, particularly those of the Communist empire in Eastern Europe. People Power manifested itself in Manila a second time in 2001 (from January 17 to January 19) with the ousting of the actor-turned-president Joseph Estrada, who was in turn replaced by Gloria Macapagal-Arroyo, daughter of former Philippine president Diosdado Macapagal.

Machismo has generally been a ruling factor in traditional Filipino society. *Sabong* (cockfighting) has been a Philippine national sport for centuries. Men typically display a fascination for bladed weapons, club-type weapons, unarmed combat, and firearms. They subscribe to an unwritten code of honor in which personal combat is the inevitable result of an affront to one's manhood. One peculiar example is the refusal to drink from another man's glass when encountering a group of men drinking at a roadside *sari-sari* (variety) store. A man is expected to accept the drink even if he does not know the person who offers it. Despite its potentially unsanitary implications, to decline such an offer would be to invite a fight, because this act supposedly insinuates that the man being offered the beverage places himself at a higher level than

Sabong (cockfighting) is a national sport of the Philippines. This blood sport pits two roosters (fitted with gaffs) against each other. The fight ends when one is either killed or simply turns and flees. Cockfights occur in pits called *galleras* almost every day in Metro Manila. They are also popular in the Visayan city of Cebu. A man referred to as the *kristo* (after the resurrected Christ, because of his outstretched and raised arms) calls the bets. Remarkably, the *kristo* can recall dozens of bets, which are placed using an intricate series of hand signals, without using a calculator or referring to written notes. It has been said that houses, automobiles, land, jewelry, and even wives have been wagered at the pits.

the one offering it. Strange as it may seem, this custom goes on today. On a trip home to Manila in 1994, I came across this very predicament and had to come up with a quick excuse not to accept the proffered drink. I ended up saying that I couldn't drink because I had an ulcer. This excuse went over well enough to save me from having to run away from or fight four guys on unfamiliar turf.

Filipinos are also very patriotic. The national anthem of the country ends with the heroic phrase *ang mamatay nang dahil sa iyo* (literally, "to die for you"), which is a reference to the Filipino's willingness to lay his or her life down for the motherland. Likewise, many traditional proverbs emphasize bravery, love for country, and adaptability (an important element of survival). *Walang mangaalipin kung walang papaalipin,* means "There are no masters if there are no willing slaves." *Ang bayaning nasusugatan nagiibayo ang tapang,* means "A hero's courage prevails when he is wounded." And *Ano man ang tugtog ay siyang isasayaw,* means "One dances to whatever music is playing," which reminds us that a person must adapt to any given situation to survive.

Chapter 4

The Visayas:
The Cradle of Arnis

Many historical sources describe the evolution and early forms of arnis in the Visayas region, which is comprised of the islands of Panay, Samar, Masbate, Leyte, Mactan, Negros, Cebu, and Bohol.

The Visayas is the cradle of the Filipino martial arts. The region reflects the highest development of these arts and the best-documented accounts of their evolution. Ilongo and Cebuano martial artists from the Visayas are known to this day for their excellence in diverse fighting disciplines— primarily arnis, but also jujitsu, judo, karate, and kung fu.

Some of earliest accounts of organized arnis training in the Philippines date back to August 14, 1920, when the Labangon Fencing Club was established in Cebu by a diverse group of stick-fighters, most notably Lorenzo (nicknamed "Tatay Ensong") and Teodoro (called "Doring") Saavedra. The members of this club represented different styles, but many specialized in the stick-and-dagger method known as *espada y daga*. It is said that there was much conflict among the members of the club; apparently, they fought like cats and dogs over the proper execution of each technique. The Labangon Fencing Club closed its doors a decade later in 1930 because of internal disputes.

On January 12, 1932, some members of the Labangon Fencing Club reorganized under the name Doce Pares Club. Notable among the club's

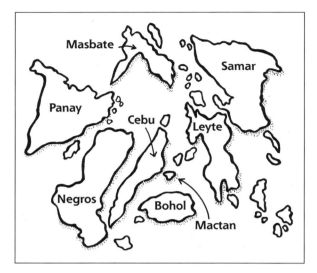

The Visayan Islands. Tiny Mactan Island is significant as the place where Ferdinand Magellan fell to the forces of chieftain Lapu Lapu.

first members were members of the renowned Canete family: Eulogio ("Yoling"), Filemon ("Momoy"), Maximo, Silvestre, Tirso, Rufino, Andres, and Ciriaco ("Cacoy"). Together with other members both old and new, the Canetes sought to develop a more organized method of training and a standard manner of executing the techniques. The Doce Pares movement would become an influential force in the worldwide dissemination of the Filipino martial arts.

Frustrated by the internal politics of the original group, Venancio "Anciong" Bacon, a top pupil of Lorenzo Saavedra, moved to another part of Cebu to establish the Balintawak Club. Balintawak was simply the name of the street where Bacon had his school, which was in the backyard of the house of one of his students, Eduardo Baculi. Bacon favored the single stick method of fighting and the use of the free hand to check an opponent's movements. His version of arnis did not use the stick-spinning maneuvers, fanning strikes, or snapping strikes widely practiced by other groups, as he considered these moves to be impractical.

Bacon's Balintawak method was more linear and direct, and it was geared to use in direct combat rather than in sports matches or public demonstrations.

The Doce Pares and Balintawak clubs soon developed a natural rivalry, with each side claiming superiority over the other; they often engaged in challenge matches to try to prove their dominance. Each side won their fare share of these encounters, and numerous offshoot clubs emerged from both clubs.

World War II mobilized tens of thousands of ordinary Filipinos into action against the invading Japanese Imperial Army. Local citizens, from common laborers to intellectuals, took up arms as guerilla fighters, conducting reconnaissance missions, gathering intelligence, staging ambushes, and providing crucial assistance to the American forces trapped in the islands. Numerous accounts describe how arnis fighters courageously served as point men in close-quarter jungle encounters.

It was also common for arnis practitioners to serve as the *berdugos* (from the Spanish word *verdugo,* meaning executioner) who beheaded the *makapili,* Filipino collaborators who identified members of the resistance to the Japanese, as well as the captured enemy soldiers. Although the beheadings may seem barbaric, it should be noted that this measure was a reaction to the atrocities exacted by the Japanese on the locals. The invaders were known to round up Filipino civilians and use them for live bayonet practice (running them through the torso with bayonets) or sword practice (cutting their heads off with their katanas).

Filipinos valiantly fought side-by-side with American forces at Bataan, Corregidor, and other crucial battles, and the Philippines suffered thousands of casualties in the process. This wartime experience had a profound effect on a whole generation of locals. To this day, many people born before 1935 use the different phases of the war—Pre-war, Occupation, and Peacetime or Liberation— as markers on the timelines of their lives. The war also gave arnis exponents an intimate understanding of actual life-or-death combat, further lending an element of reality to the art.

With the end of the war came an influx of Western goods and concepts. Filipinos readily embraced and emulated many aspects of American culture. Arnis' popularity waned as it was overshadowed by the martial arts that were rapidly catching on in the West, namely jujitsu, judo, aikido, karate, and kickboxing. Arnis practice remained strong, however, on a regional basis. Its power base was in the Visayas; its continued practice there maintained a legacy dating back to the sixteenth century.

Several groups that sprouted from the Balintawak and Doce Pares clubs continued to operate through these post-war times. These included the Balintawak International Self-Defense Club (founded in 1957), a later incarnation of Bacon's original Balintawak Club; the Durex Self-Defense Club (founded in 1959), which taught arnis, judo, and karate; the Black Cat Self-Defense Club (founded in 1966), which offered instruction in judo and arnis; the Filipinas Garote Self-Defense Club (founded in 1966), which also taught judo and arnis; the Lapunti Self-Defense Club (founded in 1972), created by Filemon Caburnay, former Doce Pares member, and Johnny Chiuten, a renowned kung fu master and direct disciple of Anciong Bacon; the Cebu Mutual Security Association Self-Defense Club (founded in 1972), which taught arnis, judo, aikido, wrestling, and karate; the Mandaue Martial Arts Club (founded in 1973), which taught arnis, judo, karate, and aikido; and the New Arnis Confederation of the Visayas and Mindanao (founded in 1975), which brought together arnis exponents from the two major island groups.

Chapter 5

The Golden Age of Arnis

By the mid-1960s most Manila residents considered arnis to be anachronistic—a rural activity or cultural-demonstration art that was inferior to the more-popular arts of karate, judo, and kung fu and practiced only by lower-class people from the provinces, slums, and back alleys or by public school students. (Public school attendees were—and still are today—generally looked down upon by aristocratic Manila residents.) Rich *mistisos* (from the Spanish *mestizos,* signifying people of mixed Filipino and Spanish, Chinese, or American parentage) practiced the foreign martial systems, while only people from the lower classes or from the provinces practiced arnis.

In the late 1960s arnis masters attempted to reintroduce the art to the general Filipino population. To do this, they had to go to Manila, where the media coverage would be the greatest and the public demonstrations would reach the most people. Alejandro Roces, the Philippine education secretary at the time, helped sponsor the Arnis Revival Movement, a drive launched by the Samahan ng Arnis sa Pilipinas (Arnis Association in the Philippines). The association's member schools presented arnis demonstrations at different venues as well as on national television.

This attempt at revival culminated in Manila's so-called Martial Arts Golden Age, which began in 1970. That year many martial arts schools opened in and around Quiapo, the heart of Manila's downtown area. Many different systems were represented, including Okinawan and Japanese karate, judo, aikido, yaw yan (a Filipino kicking art developed by Napoleon Fernandez), TRACMA (an acronym for Trovador Ramos Association of Consolidated Martial Arts, after its founder), Sikaran (also a Filipino kicking method), tat kun tao (a combination of arnis and kung fu), thai ki do (said to be a blend of Thai kickboxing and hapkido), and Ngo Cho kung fu (a previously secret art, which was gradually becoming available to Filipinos). Arnis also became distinctly visible in the capital city. Interestingly, most arnis masters teaching during this period did not build elaborate schools to increase the popularity and visibility of their systems. Most taught at the Luneta (officially Rizal Park, named after Philippine national hero José Rizal) and other parks or simply held classes in a student's house or backyard. Revisionist history written by non-Filipino writers indicates otherwise, depicting these masters as offering instruction under dojo-like conditions.

Arnis was practiced using mainly the *yantok* (yan-TOK), which are rattan sticks. This was due mainly to a strict prohibition on weapons put forth by Ferdinand Marcos when he declared martial law on September 21, 1972. It was forbidden to carry blades, but the practice of arnis with rattan sticks, according to an official government declaration, complied with the goals of the so-called New Society.

In 1974 a TV program called Karate Arnis Pilipino, created by martial arts pioneer Guillermo "Doc" Lengson, began airing on weekends. It showcased competitive full-contact karate and point arnis matches and attracted fighters from all over the country. The karate bouts consisted of three two-minute rounds and used kickboxing rules patterned after the American version of the sport that was gaining attention at the time. A notable difference was that no kicking was permitted to the head.

Competitors wore tennis shoes in the ring. The arnis matches, on the other hand, required the donning of light body armor, kendo-style headgear, and gloves, because rattan sticks were used in these matches. Winners were determined by points; they were judged based on the number of hits scored in a given time period. When the referee perceived what he believed to be a valid strike, he would stop the action, and the judges would determine the number of points to be awarded. At least one of the two side judges had to concur with the referee for a given point to count—similar to point karate tournaments.

José Bonco Presas (1907—1979), patriarch of the Presas family of arnis teachers, from an old photograph illustrating the *espada y daga* method. The elder Presas began teaching his son Ernesto at age eight. Note the full grip on the weapons and the strong forward stance, distinct characteristics of the Kombatan system.

Chapter 6

From Modern Arnis to Kombatan

Kapag ang tigre ay namatay iniiwan nito ang kanyang balat,

Kapag ang tao ay namatay iniiwan nito ang kanyang pangalan

When a tiger dies, it leaves its skin,

When a man dies, he leaves his name.

—Grandmaster Ernesto A. Presas Sr.

Manila 1971. It's an extremely hot and humid summer day. You're in the heart of the downtown business district. You walk down Claro M. Recto Avenue past the National Bookstore at the corner of Morayta and past sidewalk vendors hawking magazines, slippers, cooking utensils, and handbags. Soon you come across the long line of movie houses playing the latest local and American films. Farther down is Avenida Rizal, gateway to Chinatown. You turn left instead on Quezon Boulevard toward the famed Quiapo Catholic Church, where enterprising vendors sell fragrant *sampaguita* flower garlands, *gayuma* (love potions), *anting anting* (talismans), and native herbal remedies for all types of ailments. You descend through an underpass and emerge on the opposite end. After walking a few more steps up the road, you see a small sign on the left: Arjuken Karate Association.

31

Kombatan founder Grandmaster
Ernesto A. Presas Sr.

You climb a flight of stairs to the entrance of a modest gym. At the front is a small desk where visitors check in. To the right is a partitioned area that serves as a dressing room. You enter the main training area; as you walk across its hardwood floor, you admire the variety of weapons from Filipino, Okinawan, and Japanese martial arts hanging on one wall. A mirror lines the far wall and a heavy punching bag hangs in one corner. Free weights lay in the opposite corner. Posted near the windows that overlook the crowded sidewalk is the gym's training schedule. The windows are wide open to allow the paltry breeze inside. There is no air-conditioning and the students sweat profusely as they train. The air is filled with the clatter of sticks clashing as partners execute block-and-counter sequences. Some students practice disarming techniques with wooden knives. An instructor teaches empty-hand combat fundamentals to some new members. This is the headquarters of the organization Grandmaster Ernesto A. Presas founded only a year ago, and as you sign up, you become a potential member of the first arnis class to graduate from the new school.

When the Presas brothers moved to Manila in 1970, it marked a pivotal point for Filipino martial arts. Ernesto Presas and his brother Remy had traveled to Osaka, Japan that year to demonstrate arnis techniques at Expo '70 (a World's Fair event). Upon returning to the Philippines,

Ernesto decided to permanently reside in Manila. In the downtown area of Quiapo, he established the Arjuken (a composite of ARnis, JUjitsu, and KENdo) Karate Association, and opened his school on Quezon Boulevard. There Presas taught the arts of Modern Arnis, Shotokan karate, combat jujitsu, and Okinawan weaponry, and the Japanese fencing sport of kendo. In the next thirty years, the school would relocate only twice—once due to a building fire and once for expansion purposes—and would stay within a two-block radius of the original school both times.

Ernesto Amador Presas Sr. was born in May of 1945 in the Visayan coastal village of Hinigaran, in Negros Occidental province. His father, José Bonco Presas, was a renowned arnis fighter in their area and began teaching Ernesto the fundamentals of arnis when he was only eight years old. A capable learner, he mastered his lessons well and soon expanded his martial arts education to include other fighting systems.

In the time-honored tradition of the arnis practitioners of that era, Presas trained intensely and fought many challenge matches against other practitioners. One memorable encounter found him facing an arnis fighter from the Manila suburb of Paranaque, who wanted to test the skills of the upstart who had just moved to the city from a rural area. The two fought in the middle of a rice paddy, where movement was severely restricted and falling into thigh-deep mud was a distinct possibility. They began with a trial match to see who could disarm the other first. Using his complete knowledge of levering and disarming methods, Presas successfully took the other fighter's stick away twice in two clashes. The other fighter wasn't satisfied with this turn of events and insisted on an all-out skirmish. Presas went on to disarm his foe once more before delivering a rain of blows that knocked his opponent into the mud.

Other fights would follow, with the frequent provision that the other fighter was always the challenger—Presas did not seek conflict, but he never backed down from it either. Because his knowledge was not limited to armed combat, Presas also bested karate practitioners (fighting them bare-handed), including one opponent who fell into a nearby river after Presas pounded him with hard punches and kicks. These battles, he would later reveal, formed the basis for his comprehensive fighting system.

In 1972 Presas secured teaching positions as a physical education instructor at the University of Santo Tomas, the University of the Philippines, Far Eastern University, the Lyceum of the Philippines, and the Central Colleges of the Philippines. He also began teaching arnis at the Far Eastern Military Academy, the Philippine National Police Academy, the General Headquarters Military Police Academy, and the Officers' Schools for the Philippine Army and Air Force.

During those formative days, the Arjuken held classes from Monday through Saturday and often held special events and demonstrations on Sundays. Arnis classes featured basic group training, with students practicing blocking, striking, thrusting, and disarming techniques on each other using rattan sticks. Sparring was practiced both with and without the use of protective equipment like headgear, body armor, and gloves. Using this equipment allowed students to make hard contact, whereas sparring unprotected called for slower action and more control, especially since only rattan sticks were available (the soft foam sticks later developed in the U.S. for training and tournaments would never gain popularity in the Philippines). Instruction on the forms *(anyo)* and practice with bladed weapons were largely conducted on a one-on-one basis because of space limitations and safety concerns.

In addition to taking arnis classes, students could learn JKA-line Shotokan karate, jujitsu throwing and locking skills, Okinawan weaponry (tonfa, bo, sai, and nunchaku), and kendo. (There exists today, particularly in Australia and Canada, a system known as Arjuken karate, popularized by early Presas students. Along with the standard Shotokan kata and its emphasis on the reverse punch and front kick, this method also features dynamic foot techniques, such as the ax, crescent, hook, and spinning hook kicks usually associated with Korean kicking styles.) Presas was a firm advocate of cross-training; he believed that this better prepared the student to deal with the greatest variety of possible attacks. Visitors would often drop by to observe the training or to practice as guests of the school. Exponents of other martial arts could often be seen among the school's regular students.

The Arjuken drew converts from many systems, such as Okinawan Shorin-ryu karate (initially the prevalent karate form in Manila due to the efforts of Latino Gonzales, his sons Roberto and Rolando, and his daughter Magna), tae kwon do, judo, and other arnis styles. Presas' younger brother Roberto served as a senior instructor in the association. Some of the original members included practitioners who would later stand out as instructors and fighters: Pepe Yap, Willie Madla, Rene Tongson, Earl Villanueva, Pepito Robas, Romy Quiambao, Cristino Vasquez, Danny Diaz, Jess Arroyo, Rey Yatsu, Jess Bonso, and European arnis pioneer Jackson Cui Brocka.

Jackson Cui Brocka was considered a free spirit among the original Arjuken members and he indeed made some changes to the art as he taught it. For instance, he renamed the 12-Strike Sequence as "Seven Strikes and Five Thrusts." He moved to the U.S. in the mid-1970s after attaining *lakan* (black belt) ranking. He called his system Combat Arnis, but he was careful to maintain his ties with the Arjuken in Manila. He taught arnis and karate at a commercial martial arts school in Tacoma, Washington, then taught in Oregon, and later, in 1978, went to what was then West Germany to help spark Germans' interest in arnis. Brocka's style, in the tradition of Ernesto Presas' teachings, was very direct and power-oriented, and he emphasized hard-contact sparring with sticks. Brocka died in an accident in the mid-1980s.

The implementation of widespread instruction and the influences from the West brought about a need to make some changes to the art and practice of arnis. Presas introduced several important innovations in his early years of teaching. He organized a standard curriculum that was effective for teaching large groups of students. The program included basic striking, blocking, and countering patterns, and effective footwork and angling techniques. Prior to this standardization, arnis practice largely consisted of undisciplined and disorganized milling about (known as *bara bara*), during which students haphazardly swung their sticks and often struck each other in sensitive areas like the fingers, wrists, forearms, elbows, and face. A teacher taught more by instinct and simply showed the students whatever he felt like demonstrating at the time. He might just hand a student a stick and order him to defend himself against the teacher's strikes—a painful learning process. Little concern was given to safety or to the practitioner's longevity in the art. This resulted in low morale and a high dropout rate, and only the most dedicated students remained long enough to truly learn the art.

Presas also influenced the Filipino martial arts uniform now in wide use. Although some consider the wearing of uniforms to be a more modern innovation influenced by judo and karate, practitioners of arnis— despite belonging to different training groups—have naturally dressed in similar fashion for years. Donning similar clothing brought about a sense of unity. It instilled a certain mindset in the practitioner that once the uniform was on, it was time to set other concerns aside and concentrate fully on training. A standard uniform was also selected to allow the freedom of movement required by the particular system practiced.

A contemporary arnis uniform and Kombatan uniform patches.

Prior to 1970 arnis practitioners wore a variety of uniforms. Some simply practiced and performed in loose-fitting civilian clothes or wore khaki pants and t-shirts. Some wore karate gi. Some wore red pants known as *kundiman* (after the pants worn in a native dance) and t-shirts. Some wore sweat suits as a nod to Bruce Lee, even though the weather in the Philippines is often too hot and humid for sweats; some preferred sweat pants with tank tops. Finally, some wore karate pants with Moro-style vests. The Filipino martial arts uniform of a karate-style top cut short at the waist and loose-fitting pants was an early Presas design. He also devised distinctive patches to better identify his organization's members. The complete uniform was usually reserved for public demonstrations, level testing, and formal occasions—it is simply too hot and humid in the Philippines to don the full attire for everyday practice. For daily training, practitioners instead wear the loose-fitting pants with t-shirts.

Presas instituted a ranking system based on colored belts to plainly identify the ability level each student had achieved. This originally consisted of three ranks: *likas* (green belt), *likha* (brown belt), and *lakan* (black belt). The *lakan* stage has ten degrees, from *lakan isa* (first degree) to *lakan sampu* (tenth degree). He also began awarding certificates indicating the given practitioner's rank. Instructors were known by the title *guro,* a designation that was originally used for schoolteachers in academic institutions but soon became widely used in Filipino martial arts circles.

The Arjuken was very active in promoting various martial arts, especially arnis, through numerous public demonstrations. One particularly notable demonstration was held at the Rizal Memorial Coliseum in 1975 during an Asian karate championship tournament attended by Goju-Kai karate master Gogen "The Cat" Yamaguchi (a superstar in Japanese karate circles). Many other events followed, including demonstrations at military bases, universities, churches, and local festivals.

Presas' pioneering efforts also gave rise to the First Intercollegiate Karate-Arnis Tournament, held in 1975 at the University of Santo Tomas' gymnasium. Participants included the University of Santo Tomas, the University of the Philippines, the Lyceum of the Philippines, and the Far Eastern University. Arjuken fighters from UST swept the championships in both the arnis and karate categories.

By 1977 Presas had begun traveling to the U.S. to teach arnis. In 1981 he wrote his first book, entitled *The Art of Arnis.* He went on to establish branches in the U.S., Australia, New Zealand, England, Germany, Denmark, Sweden, Norway, Switzerland, Austria, Finland, Canada, Mexico, Puerto Rico, the Dominican Republic, Jamaica, Israel, Saudi Arabia,

Japan, Thailand, India, and South Africa. He also created the International Philippine Martial Arts Federation (IPMAF), a monitoring and promotional organization that linked his followers worldwide. The First IPMAF Arnis Tournament and Congress, also thanks to Presas' efforts, was held on April 20, 1989 at the University of Santo Tomas in Manila. This event featured such distinguished guests as José Mena, founder one of the first established arnis schools in Manila (in the tough slum district of Tondo); Ciriaco and Dionisio Canete of the Doce Pares Club; Benjamin Luna Lema of lightning scientific arnis; Antonio Ilustrisimo of kalis ilustrisimo; and the famed Tortal brothers of pekiti tirsia.

Presas has taught tens of thousands of students, many at his headquarters in Manila and others at biannual training camps held at Presas Beach on his native island of Negros. Others yet have received training at the numerous open clinics and workshops Presas conducts at branch schools on six continents. He has influenced and gained the admiration of many outstanding instructors, including Kosho-ryu kempo headmaster Bruce Juchnik and noted combat expert Hock Hochheim. In addition, he has contributed a full line of books that present valuable information on his form of arnis, Kombatan.

Kombatan Defined

Controversy typically arises when the term Modern Arnis is mentioned in American martial arts circles. Modern Arnis, in fact, was originally a loose term used to denote the fighting art brought to Manila in 1970 by the Presas brothers Ernesto, Remy, and Roberto from their native island of Negros. Shortly after Remy moved to the United States in 1975, he received press coverage in which he was dubbed the "Father of Modern Arnis," leading people to believe that he was solely responsible for developing the system known as Modern Arnis. In the meantime, Ernesto and Roberto remained in Manila teaching their respective methods, also under the term Modern Arnis.

In order to avoid confusion and best distinguish his art, Ernesto Presas put his method through a series of name changes in the late 1980s. One designation was Arnis, Presas Style, but because Presas is a shared surname, it did not properly identify Ernesto's method. He ultimately decided on the name Kombatan (KOM-bah-tan), a title signifying a system of total combat that embraces stick, blade, and empty-hand components. (However, because he taught his art under the name Modern Arnis for several years, some of Ernesto Presas' early graduates possess certificates bearing the Modern Arnis designation.)

In the 1980s and 1990s wildly exaggerated rumors of a feud between Ernesto, Remy, and Roberto circulated among uninformed Modern Arnis practitioners. To the best of my knowledge, the three actually had a fairly strong relationship; quibbles were unavoidable, but no major feuds divided them. Ernesto unfailingly expressed his affection for his two brothers in his numerous published works. Most current practitioners of Kombatan and Modern Arnis share a camaraderie not commonly found among exponents of related systems; they freely train together and attend one another's events.

Several features distinguish Kombatan from other arnis systems. One is the use of longer and deeper stances associated with an older style of arnis. These stances facilitate the powerful execution of the techniques by providing a solid base. Another is the use of a full grip when holding the different weapons. This strong grip allows you to deliver powerful techniques while minimizing the possibility that you will drop the weapon or have it knocked out of your hand. Additionally, in Kombatan a ninety-degree angle is maintained between the weapon and the practitioner's arm to lock the weapon in place with the practitioner's body, thereby creating an uninterrupted line along which to deliver great force. Each strike essentially travels up from the feet through the legs, waist, and trunk, and out along the arm into the weapon itself.

Kombatan emphasizes using powerful strikes to end a confrontation as quickly as possible. Lastly, Kombatan features a distinct wind-up— the practitioner retracts the weapon prior to delivering the strike to generate more force.

Current Trends

If we trace the succession of the most popular martial arts traditions in the United States, we can establish a basic trend:

1950s—judo
1960s—karate
1970s—kung fu
1980s—ninjutsu, full-contact karate, tae kwon do
1990s—Brazilian jujitsu

For several reasons, arnis has not achieved (and is not likely to achieve) wide popularity in the Western world. First of all, there is the notion in Western society that armed combat is by nature "dirty fighting." Secondly, there are many laws restricting the carrying and use of weapons (which, incidentally, affects only law-abiding citizens and not the criminals).

Some people may indeed have the opinion that weapons are evil instruments. In taking an objective look, however, one would logically come to the conclusion that most implements are neutral; they are neither good nor bad. A stick or knife just lying on the ground will not get up and attack a human being. Both have practical uses beyond striking or cutting an opponent. A stick can be used to hold a car hatch open, to beat a dusty carpet, or as an aid in walking. A knife can be used to cut rope, slice vegetables, or open a box. It is the intention and action of the wielder that ultimately determines whether a certain object is utilized for good or bad purposes.

When used for legitimate self-defense purposes, weapons greatly enhance one's chances of surviving an attack. Weapons may be particularly valuable against a considerably larger foe, a group of assailants, or an armed individual (when bare-handed techniques are less ideal). This has often been the case in the Philippines, where concepts of fair play do not figure in to many combative situations, especially in the cowardly sneak attack *(pa-traidor)* or the free-for-all fight *(labo labo* or *bakbakan).* Furthermore, the presence of a weapon could itself act as a deterrent against an attack in certain cases.

Another explanation for arnis' lack of popularity in the West is that there are few schools dedicated exclusively to teaching Filipino martial arts. Arnis was first introduced to the U.S., and to the rest of the Western world, as a "seminar" art or an "add-on" system—something to complement the empty-handed techniques of other martial arts. Many of the first non-Filipino practitioners of arnis were karate, kenpo, and tae kwon do stylists, who learned arnis through short seminars only. It is no secret that after its initial exposure in the 1970s, arnis became the weaponry component of several kenpo systems. (This was fostered by the fact that many arnis movements were compatible with the elaborate hand techniques of the kenpo styles.)

Arnis has yet to escape the seminar mode of instruction. It is, unfortunately, still largely disseminated the world over as a "complementary" method. This has led to the modern phenomenon of some practitioners being versed in drills and exercises but lacking the more profound hands-on experience past practitioners possessed.

In contrast, original arnis practitioners had deep knowledge and insight based on intensive and sometimes dangerous training. They often had skills gleaned from practicing and sparring with exponents from a variety of systems, some friendly and some hostile. They also had a certain hardiness, which came from training with little or no protective equipment to spare them from bumps and bruises. Although using protective equipment is necessary for safe training, particularly in today's litigious world, being too reliant on it has led instructors to produce a new breed of arnis practitioners who can execute dazzling movements worthy of a demonstration but are unable to apply their art in real-life, unrestrained, and unchoreographed situations.

Only through a concerted effort can arnis be propagated on a larger scale and still remain true to the teachings of its founders. This may prove difficult, as the diverse Filipino movements and groups are largely averse to coming together under a common leadership. The spirit of independence that gave rise to arnis has also served to deter its effective dissemination outside of the Philippines. The different groups have nonetheless made some progress in teaching their respective methods on a relatively widespread basis. The International Philippine Martial Arts Federation, for example, has established a dedicated body of practitioners in several countries and holds training camps at Presas Beach on the island of Negros every other year. The Doce Pares association has sponsored several major international tournaments. Perhaps it is the efforts of these organizations that will determine whether true arnis survives.

Part Two

The Practice

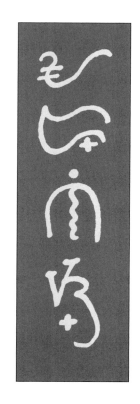

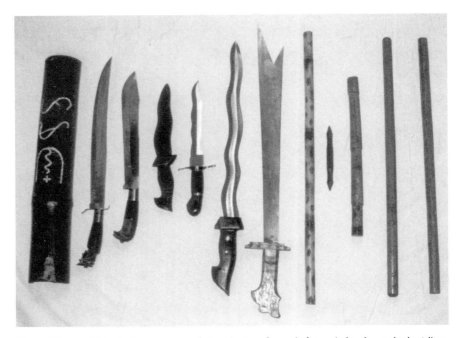

The sticks and bladed weapons of Kombatan from left to right: long *bolo (dina-hong palay)*, medium *bolo*, wooden *daga*, metal *daga*, *kris*, *kampilan*, rattan *yantok*, *dulo dulo*, shorter rattan *yantok*, *kamagong yantok*, and *bahi yantok*. The last two sticks are made of hardwoods that are extremely dense and heavy.

The Weapons of Kombatan

The armed component of Kombatan utilizes a number of sticks and bladed weapons. The sticks include: the *yantok* (also called *baston* or *garote*), with standard lengths ranging from twenty-four to twenty-eight inches; the *dulo dulo,* a short stick similar in use to the Japanese *yawara* stick that measures about seven inches and is held in the palm of the hand; and the *bangkaw,* or six-foot-long staff. There is also the wooden *daga,* about fourteen inches in length, which can be a simple round stick or be shaped like a fighting knife.

Shorter bladed weapons include the metal version of the *daga* and the *balisong* (the Filipino fan knife), the handle of which has sections that swivel to form a sheath around the blade. Longer blades include the *bolo,* a common farm implement in the rural Philippines; the *binakoko,* a long blade named after the porgy fish; the *barang,* a flat-headed blade; the *dinahong palay,* named after a poisonous snake; the *kris,* a sword used in the Islamic southern provinces that sometimes has a wavy blade; and the *kampilan,* also popular in the Islamic south, which has one blade with a forked tip.

The weapons of the body include the fists, open hands, forearms, elbows, knees, shins, feet, and head. Although anatomical weapons are not commonly viewed as weapons at all, their proper development is regarded as being of equal importance to proficiency with the stick and bladed implements.

Chapter 7

The Foundation

"Paganito po ba?"

"Hindi, paganito"

"This way, sir?"

"No, this way."

Stances

A good stance *(pagtayo)* provides the foundation for the powerful and effective execution of offensive and defensive maneuvers. Some stances also serve as transitional positions, allowing you to safely move from defensive mode to attack mode and vice versa.

Some arnis systems do not use standard terms to describe their stances. When teaching, instructors of such systems might say, "To attack, move one foot forward about two paces from the rear foot, bend the front knee, place most of your weight on that front leg, and keep the rear leg straight or nearly straight. You can also lift the heel of the rear foot. Make sure both legs are no less than shoulder-width apart so you can maintain a solid base." The Kombatan instructor, on the other hand, would simply say, "Forward stance." Using terms that are universally familiar to martial arts practitioners simplifies the learning process. Here are the most commonly used stances in the Kombatan system.

Forward Stance. This stance is generally used for offense. Move one foot forward about two paces in front of the other foot. Bend your front knee and place seventy percent of your body weight on your front leg. Keep your rear leg straight or nearly straight. You can lift the heel of the rear foot slightly. Keep both legs shoulder-width apart to maintain a strong base. The forward stance is used to bridge the distance between you and your opponent, allowing you to reach him or her with your weapon.

Back Stance. The back stance allows you to defend against an opponent's aggressive strikes and to launch a counterattack. Bend the knee of your rear leg, and place sixty percent of your weight on that leg. Keep the front leg bent to avoid a incurring a knee injury from a kicking attack to that area. The back stance may also be used in conjunction with the cat stance for better defensive maneuvering.

Horse Stance. Used primarily for fielding attacks from the side, the horse stance limits the number of vulnerable targets on you by exposing only one side of your body to your opponent. Stand with your legs two shoulder-widths apart and bend your knees. The horse stance is a very stable position and is effective for standing your ground in the face of a strong attack. It can be used in conjunction with a forward stance to execute a counterattack.

Cat Stance. This is a short stance that allows for quick, light movements. Place one foot about a half-pace in front of the other and bend both legs. The front foot touches the ground lightly with the toes or the ball of the foot and bears only ten percent of your body weight. The cat stance may be used to quickly retract from a frontal attack when there is not enough time to take a full step back.

Cross Stance. This stance serves as both a transitional position with which to angle away from an opponent's advances and a base from which to launch a counterattack. Place one foot ahead of the other, and turn the front foot out, so that it's at a right angle to the rear foot. A right cross stance has the right foot facing right and vice versa. The front foot bears seventy percent of your body weight.

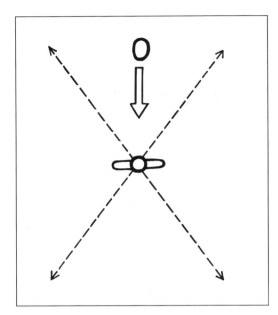

X Step Pattern.

Footwork and Body Angling

Proper footwork *(hakbang)* has many uses; it is paramount to being a well-rounded fighter. With good footwork, you can easily avoid an opponent's offensive efforts. You can move into range quickly to reach an opponent with a short weapon. You can also position yourself to one side to use a longer weapon at close range.

Kombatan footwork patterns were derived from traditional Filipino dances, such as the *Dandansoy,* the *Itik Itik,* and the *Sakuting,* the latter of which uses two sticks reminiscent of the *doble baston* technique discussed in Chapter Eight. The two major components of Kombatan footwork are the "X" step and the "L" step. You can use these moves to evade an opponent's attack without making large stepping movements—you simply angle the body out of the line of fire using small motions. Used together, the X step and the L step comprise the asterisk symbol, which is the Universal Angles of Motion Pattern described below placed on a vertical plane.

X Step. This method of body angling places the practitioner at forward and backward diagonal angles. By using these angles, you can execute blocks, parries, counters, and evasive techniques against an opponent's offensive efforts.

Right Front Diagonal Step.

Left Front Diagonal Step.

Right Back Diagonal Step.

Left Back Diagonal Step.

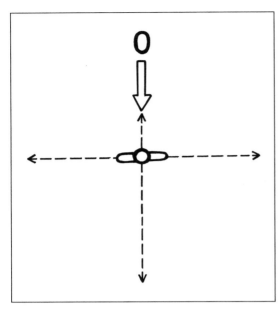

L Step Pattern.

L Step. This method of body angling places the practitioner at ninety-degree angles, both sideways and straight backward and forward. It allows you to execute blocks, parries, counters, evasive techniques, and offensive techniques against an opponent.

Right Step.

Left Step.

Back Step.

Front Step.

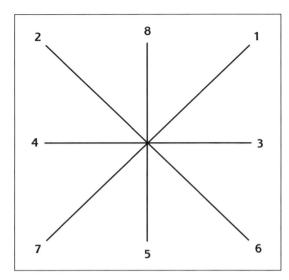

The Universal Angles of Motion Pattern.

Universal Angles of Motion Pattern

This pattern represents all the various angles that an attack could pass through. It is not meant to illustrate fixed techniques against specific targets. Indeed, the target and the weapon used may change while the angle remains the same. A strike along the first angle, for instance, may be delivered to an opponent's temple, neck, hand, wrist, elbow, hip, knee, or ankle (if you are kneeling). A strike along the fourth angle may be directed toward the same targets by simply adjusting your stance. A strike along the eighth angle may be directed at the opponent's crown, collarbone, forearm, or virtually any part of his or her body if he or she is in a prone position. Each particular strike may also be delivered with a number of different weapons and with different portions of those weapons.

By studying this pattern, you also reduce the number of defenses you must learn to effectively block and counter an opponent's attack. All attacks traveling along the eighth angle, for example, can be dealt with in similar manner, making some allowances for the type of weapon involved.

A strike to wrist, a thrust to eye, and a pommel blow to the face, all delivered along the same angle.

A strike to face, a reverse thrust to eye, and a reverse-grip thrust to the neck, all delivered along the same angle.

Anatomical Targets

If you wildly swing a stick or slash at an opponent with a knife, you can, of course, expect to cause at least some damage to virtually any part of the human body; however, if you attack certain vital points, you will yield much greater results. Below I describe the most common anatomical targets and the typical techniques used to attack them.

Crown of the head: Descending strikes and pommel blows (strikes using the bottom end or handle of a stick or bladed weapon). Descending elbow strikes or hammer fist strikes (the hammer fist is the meaty portion on the little-finger end of a closed fist).

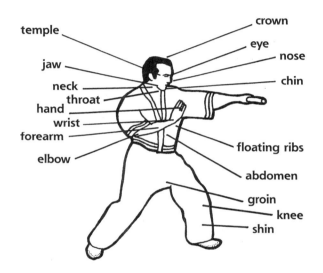

The body's targets.

Eyes: Penetrating thrusts with a stick or bladed weapon. Spear hand strikes with the fingertips.

Nose: Downward diagonal or inward strikes with a stick. Pommel blows with a stick or bladed weapon. Straight punches, hooking punches, or back-fist strikes with the fists. Inside strikes with the elbows.

Jaw: Downward diagonal or inward strikes with a stick. Pommel blows with a stick or bladed weapon. Straight or hooking punches with the fists. Inside strikes with the elbows.

Chin: Inward strikes with a stick. Pommel blows with a stick or bladed weapon. Straight punches, hooking punches, or uppercuts with the fists. Inside strikes with the elbows.

nape of neck

spine

back of knee

The body's targets.

Neck: Downward diagonal or inward strikes with a stick or bladed weapon. Penetrating thrusts with a stick or bladed weapon.

Nape of the Neck: Downward diagonal or inward strikes with a stick or bladed weapon. Direct downward strikes or pommel blows with a stick or bladed weapon on an opponent who is bending forward from the waist. Descending blows with the elbows, hammer fists, or heels of the feet on an opponent who is bending forward.

Throat: Penetrating thrusts or horizontal strikes with a stick or bladed weapon. Spear hand strikes with the fingertips.

Elbow: Downward diagonal or inward strikes with a stick or bladed weapon. Arm-breaking techniques applied by grabbing the wrist and striking the extended elbow with a forearm.

Forearm: Downward diagonal or inward strikes with a stick or bladed weapon. Strikes with the forearms that are executed while blocking an opponent's aggressive actions.

Wrist: Downward vertical, downward diagonal, or inward strikes with a stick or bladed weapon. Pommel blows with a stick or bladed weapon.

Hand: Downward vertical, downward diagonal, or inward strikes with a stick or bladed weapon. Pommel blows with a stick or bladed weapon.

Abdomen: Penetrating thrusts with a stick or bladed weapon. Straight punches, hooking punches, or uppercuts with the fists. Front kicks, side kicks, or roundhouse kicks. Knee strikes.

Floating Ribs: Horizontal strikes with a stick or bladed weapon. Pommel blows with a stick or bladed weapon. Hooking punches or uppercuts with the fists. Front kicks, side kicks, or roundhouse kicks. Knee strikes.

Spine: Horizontal strikes or descending strikes with a stick on an opponent who is bending forward. Straight punches, hooks, or uppercuts with the fists. Elbow strikes and knee strikes. Front kicks or side kicks.

Groin: Forward or upward thrusts with a stick or bladed weapon. Uppercuts with the fists. Palm slaps and grab-and-tear techniques. Front kicks, side kicks, or roundhouse kicks.

Knee: Downward diagonal or horizontal strikes with a stick or bladed weapon. Side kicks or roundhouse kicks.

Back of Knee: Strong side kicks that will cause a takedown.

Shin: Downward diagonal or horizontal strikes with a stick or bladed weapon. Side kicks.

Dead Zones

Dead zones are areas of relative safety from which a practitioner can deliver disabling offensive techniques with minimal threat of retaliation from his or her opponent. These zones become momentarily available when you properly time your footwork and movements in relation to those of your opponent.

There are two areas to be aware of when looking for dead zones—one is outside your opponent's arms and the other is inside his arms, within reach of both of his hands. Positioning yourself in the area outside your opponent's arms is generally safer, because it limits his or her capacity to follow up or counterattack. However, certain situations may dictate that you position yourself inside your opponent's arms—not getting stuck while in that area becomes a matter of timing.

For example, to move inside an attack, you can do the following: As your opponent prepares to deliver a forehand strike, charge in at an angle (to the right) while covering his weapon-wielding arm with your second hand (the empty hand that is not holding a weapon), and deliver a forehand strike or pommel blow to his face. Be sure to time your movement so that he doesn't actually have the chance to extend his strike—blocking his stick with your arm could result in a broken forearm. If you do not have time to move in before his arm extends, you can instead wait for the strike to pass through before countering (this is described more in the next technique).

Moving inside.

If you are far enough away from your opponent that you cannot safely move in without being struck by his stick, first allow him to swing the weapon inward, and lean back to avoid the blow. Before your opponent can bring his stick back for a backhand strike, charge in while covering his weapon-wielding arm. As you do so, deliver a backhand strike or pommel blow to his head.

Moving outside and countering.

As your opponent prepares to deliver a backhand strike, charge in at an angle to the left, covering his weapon-wielding arm with your second hand, and deliver a backhand strike or pommel blow to his head.

Moving outside.

If you are at a distance where you cannot safely move in without being struck by your opponent's stick, first allow him to swing the weapon outward, and lean back to avoid the blow. Before he can bring the stick back for a forehand strike, charge in while covering his weapon-wielding arm, and deliver a forehand strike or pommel blow to his face.

Moving outside and countering.

Chapter 8

Stick Combat

Solo Baston: The Heart of the Matter

Solo baston, the art of single-stick combat, is the starting point for arnis training. Through *solo baston,* the student learns the vital offensive and defensive angles; striking, thrusting, and pommel techniques; blocking and parrying; and disarming methods. These skills

translate into proficiency in a multitude of weapons techniques and technical categories. *Solo baston* also forms the foundation for the use of paired weapons, such as the *doble baston* (double stick) and *espada y daga* (sword and dagger) combinations.

It is said that the stick was brought into use because of a prohibition on bladed weapons during Spanish colonial times, but that does not mean it is an inferior weapon. The stick is a formidable fighting implement with features that actually make it superior to the blade. First of all, both ends of the stick can be held using the same grip. Secondly, unlike the knife or *bolo,* the stick can readily be used in less dangerous situations— it is not as visually threatening as a knife. Lastly, it is less dangerous in the hands of an unskilled attacker. If your opponent manages to take your weapon from you, you'll be in far less danger if that weapon is a stick instead of a blade.

Different Filipino martial arts systems use sticks of different lengths. Groups that emphasize close-quarter combat sometimes favor a shorter stick of about twenty-four inches in length, whereas other groups prefer longer ones of up to thirty-six inches in length. Kombatan students typically begin training with twenty-eight-inch sticks but eventually learn to utilize others of different lengths, taking into consideration that in an actual combat situation one may not wind up with a stick of his or her preferred length.

The most dangerous part of stick is the top third of the shaft; however, each end is a business end, with the top tip used for thrusting applications and the bottom tip used for pommel blows.

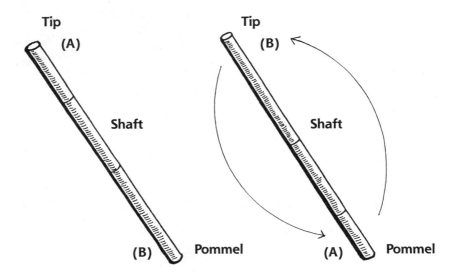

Stick anatomy. An advantage of the stick over the knife or bolo is that the stick can be held at either end and used to strike, thrust, or deliver pommel blows.

The Philippine government has recognized the effectiveness of the stick, and riot squads are commonly equipped with rattan sticks and shields in situations that do not warrant the use of firearms.

Gripping Fundamentals

A proper grip *(paghawak)* is vital to the successful delivery of a weapons technique. Kombatan uses a full grip in stick-fighting for greater stability and power. This position resembles a standard closed fist, with the stick held in the palm of the hand. Wrap your thumb and fingers completely around the stick. Maintain a firm grip, but don't grasp the stick too tightly or fatigue will set in and you will ultimately lose control of your weapon. Conversely, do not grasp the stick too loosely or you will be unable to deliver effective strikes and may drop the weapon.

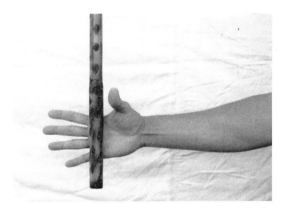 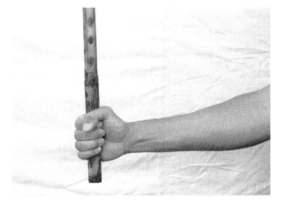

A full grip.

Don't hold your thumb up and away from the body of the stick, because this will inevitably lead to a loss of control—the weapon will get knocked out of your hand in a hard clash. Do not extend your thumb along the shaft, because this leaves the thumb exposed to a painful and potentially disabling hit. Also, don't extend either the index finger or middle finger for the same reason.

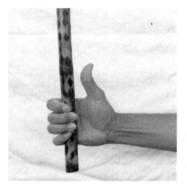  

Examples of weaker grips.

Hold the stick so that the pommel extends at least one inch—but not more than two inches—below your little finger. If you let the pommel extend too far, you could hit or hook your own wrist in the process of manipulating the stick. Hold it too close to the end and the stick could slip out of your grasp.

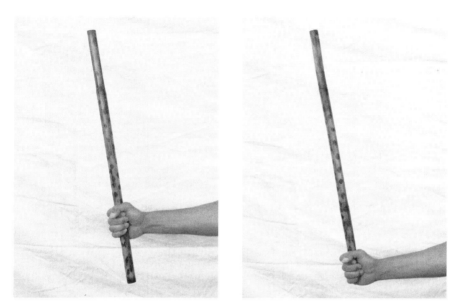

Examples of improper pommel extensions.

Always maintain a ninety-degree (or near ninety-degree) alignment between your forearm and the stick when delivering strikes, thrusts, and pommel blows. This guarantees that the stick is properly locked in your hand, which will allow you to deliver powerful and decisive blows.

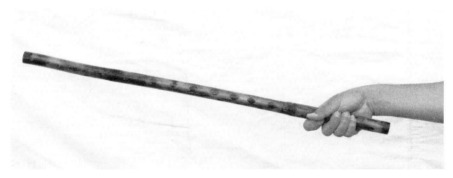

Weak wrist position.

Remember that a dropped weapon, be it a stick or other weapon, could mean a lost life. Maintaining a proper and solid grip on your weapon during training increases your chances of emerging victorious from a real confrontation.

Generating Power

Kombatan is primarily a straightforward and power-oriented arnis system. Its main philosophy is that you must end a confrontation as quickly as possible. The longer a fight goes on, the greater the possibility that you will sustain major injuries. To generate the type of power that can end a fight quickly and decisively, Kombatan uses a distinct wind-up that loads and releases a strike in an explosive fashion. The practitioner draws the stick back and delivers the technique powerfully by executing a sharp turn of the hips in the direction of the strike. While this approach is criticized by some as being telegraphic in nature and thus easy to counter, it better conforms to the reality of combat. In actual combat, a flicking or glancing blow is nearly as useless as a total miss. The exceptions to this rule are the abaniko and pilantik methods, which are snapping patterns of movement; they are meant to be set-up maneuvers that distract your opponent, allowing you to deliver stronger blows.

Power execution.

An effective second hand position.

Second Hand Basics

The second hand *(kabilang kamay)* is the empty hand not holding a weapon. For right-handed people wielding a stick with the right hand, the second hand would be the left hand. Kombatan uses a specific second hand configuration: the hand is held open, vertical, and close to one's centerline. The second hand may move slightly in the direction of the weapon as it comes into play—this movement facilitates checking or trapping maneuvers.

Other second hand positions exist, though they may provide lesser degrees of protection and effectiveness. Below are some of the more common ones.

Palm on chest. This position can slow you down, because you must turn your hand over before you bring it into play. Don't worry about checking your heartbeat during combat—you can do this afterward!

Overextended. This position exposes the arm of your second hand to hits from your opponent.

Too far back. This position renders the second hand useless for checking or trapping. While this placement is common in sport fencing, arnis is not primarily a sport and does not have built-in safeguards for its combatants.

Karate chamber. This position also renders the second hand useless. Holding the hand in a fist by the ribs immobilizes it. Moving it into play from this position will waste precious seconds that you may need to effectively check or trap your opponent's weapon.

Other second hand positions.

Forehand Diagonal Strike.

Forehand Diagonal Thrust.

Forehand Diagonal Pommel.

Stick Work: Strikes, Thrusts, and Pommel Blows

Strikes *(hampas or palo)*, thrusts *(saksak)*, and pommel blows *(bayo)* represent the three main operations performed with the stick. Each type of technique may be delivered along the horizontal, vertical, and diagonal lines in the Universal Angles of Motion Pattern. The various applications of each may be found in established patterns like the 12-Strike Sequence and patterns of movement like the krusada, banda banda, and rompida. Below are explanations of the primary stick techniques.

Forehand Diagonal Strike. Start in a high forehand position (holding the stick near the right ear), and strike inward along a downward diagonal angle. This is the most instinctive way to strike with a stick; even untrained individuals use this strike in combat. Targets include the temples, shoulders, forearms, wrists, hands, and knees.

Forehand Diagonal Thrust. Start in a high forehand position, and thrust inward along a downward diagonal angle. Targets include the eyes and the throat.

Forehand Diagonal Pommel. Start in a high forehand position, and use the pommel of the stick to strike inward along a downward diagonal angle. Targets include the temples, nose, and jaw.

Backhand Diagonal Strike. Start in a high backhand position (holding the stick near the left ear), and strike outward along a downward diagonal angle. Targets include the temples, shoulders, forearms, wrists, hands, and knees.

Backhand Diagonal Thrust. Start in a high backhand position, and thrust outward along a downward diagonal angle. Targets include the eyes and the throat.

Backhand Diagonal Pommel. Start in a high backhand position, and use the pommel of the stick to strike outward along a downward diagonal angle. Targets include the temples, nose, and jaw.

Backhand Diagonal Strike.

Backhand Diagonal Thrust.

Backhand Diagonal Pommel.

Forehand Horizontal Strike.

Forehand Horizontal Thrust.

Forehand Horizontal Pommel.

Forehand Horizontal Strike. Start in a middle forehand position (holding the stick near the right shoulder), and strike inward along a horizontal angle. Targets include the chin, shoulders, floating ribs, forearms, wrists, hands, and (if you are kneeling) the knees and shins.

Forehand Horizontal Thrust. Start in a middle forehand position, and thrust inward along a horizontal angle. Targets include the throat, eyes, underarms, abdomen, and groin.

Forehand Horizontal Pommel. Start in a middle forehand position, and strike inward along a horizontal angle using the pommel of the stick. Targets include the jaw and floating ribs.

Backhand Horizontal Strike. Start in a middle backhand position (holding the stick near the left shoulder), and strike outward along a horizontal angle. Targets include the chin, shoulders, floating ribs, forearms, wrists, hands, and (if you are kneeling) the knees and shins.

Backhand Horizontal Thrust. Start in a middle backhand position, and thrust outward along a horizontal angle. Targets include the eyes, throat, underarms, and abdomen.

Backhand Horizontal Pommel. Start in a middle backhand position, and strike outward along a horizontal angle using the pommel of the stick. Targets include the throat, jaw, and floating ribs.

Backhand Horizontal Strike.

Backhand Horizontal Thrust.

Backhand Horizontal Pommel.

Forward Thrust.

Forward Thrust. Hold the stick near your right hip and deliver a straight thrust. Targets include the throat, underarms, and midsection.

Downward Strike. Start in a high forehand position, and deliver a downward strike. Targets include the crown of the head, the nape of the neck (if your opponent is bending forward), and the forearms, wrists, and hands.

Downward Strike.

Downward Pommel. Start in a high forehand position, and deliver a downward strike using the pommel of the stick. Targets include the crown of the head, the nape of the neck (if your opponent is bending forward), and the forearms, wrists, and hands.

Downward Pommel.

The 12-Strike Sequence

There are many numbering systems in arnis; they are designed to teach the rudiments of stick work and combined strikes, and they explain sequences that include anywhere from five to sixty-four strikes. The most common grouping, used by many arnis systems, consists of twelve techniques. The first five techniques are often identical from school to school, a legacy of the original *cinco teros* (from the Spanish *cinco tiros,* meaning "five strikes") of classical arnis, which has been elaborated upon by succeeding practitioners.

The sequence described below comes from the Presas family line of arnis and is practiced by Modern Arnis and Kombatan exponents everywhere. Note that although the techniques are initially practiced with the stick, the same movements may be executed with a long-bladed weapon like a *bolo* or sword. Using bladed weapons instead of sticks would, of course, yield different results—strikes that would only produce bumps, bruises, or broken bones with the stick would cause decapitation, dismemberment, or disembowelment if done with live blades. For example, the Number Twelve Strike could behead an opponent if it was used on him as he bent forward. A Number One Strike could dismember an opponent if it hits the forearm of his weapon-wielding arm.

Number One Strike. Deliver a forehand strike along a downward diagonal angle to your opponent's left temple.

Number Two Strike. Deliver a backhand strike along a downward diagonal aimed to your opponent's right temple. It can serve as a follow-up if the Number One Strike misses its target.

Number Three Strike. Deliver a forehand horizontal strike to the tip of your opponent's left shoulder. You can think of this strike as a variation of the Number One Strike that travels on a different plane.

Number Four Strike. Deliver a backhand horizontal strike to the tip of your opponent's right shoulder. It can serve as a follow-up if the Number Three Strike misses its target.

Number Five Strike. Deliver a penetrating thrust to your opponent's abdominal area.

Number Six Strike. Deliver a forehand diagonal thrust to your opponent's left pectoral area. If it comes from an outside angle, this thrust can be difficult to block.

The 12-Strike Sequence.

Number Seven Strike. Deliver a backhand horizontal thrust to your opponent's right pectoral area. This move belongs to the "reverse" category of techniques; reverse techniques may not be as powerful as standard ones, but they're often effective because the opponent has a hard time detecting the movement in time to block it.

Number Eight Strike. Deliver a downward and outward diagonal strike to either of your opponent's knees. This is a version of the Number Two Strike, delivered to a lower target.

Number Nine Strike. Deliver a downward and inward diagonal strike to either of your opponent's knees. This is a version of the Number One Strike, delivered to a lower target.

Number Ten Strike. Deliver an inward thrust to your opponent's left eye. Even if this injury isn't devastating, it will affect the opponent's sight enough to give you the advantage.

Number Eleven Strike. Deliver a reverse thrust to your opponent's right eye. This move also aims to disable the opponent by reducing his field of vision.

Number Twelve Strike. Deliver a heavy downward strike to your opponent's crown. Use your momentum and your body weight to generate a lethal descending force.

The 12-Strike Sequence.

Blocks and Deflections

A fundamental principle of blocking consists simply of making an "X" or a "+" symbol when your weapon or forearm clashes against your opponent's weapon or forearm. Achieving this ninety-degree (or near-ninety-degree) angle ensures maximum cover and safety. Note the X or + alignments in the following photos and how they allow the defender to effectively thwart his opponent's attack. If you follow this basic principle, you can defend yourself against any offensive movement without knowing or following formal blocking methods. Furthermore, each block *(sangga* or *salag)* may also be used to hit the opponent's weapon-wielding hand or wrist to instantly disarm him or her.

Blocks and deflections are most effective when utilized in conjunction with body angling, especially when an opponent is attacking with a heavy stick that can deliver a disabling strike *(hambalos)*. An X step or L step is executed to the opposite side of the attack to nullify it. If there is not enough time to actually take a step, the practitioner can simply lean his body in the opposite direction for equal effect.

The six blocks illustrated below are the standard blocks in the Kombatan repertoire. They cover every conceivable angle of attack you might face. Start each block from a right forward stance, and hold your stick in front of your body in a horizontal position.

Number One Block: Inward.

Number One Block: Inward. Sweep the stick inward and across the body (keep the stick vertical or nearly vertical). If you anticipate a very powerful strike from your opponent (i.e., he or she has a heavier stick), you can brace your stick near the pommel with the palm of your second hand. Otherwise, an unsupported block is generally sufficient to stop an attack. The Number One Block and Catch is used against the Number One, Three, Six, and Ten strikes (forehand strikes and thrusts) of the 12-Strike Sequence.

Number Two Block: Outward. Sweep the stick outward, keeping it vertical or nearly so. You can also brace the stick with the palm of your second hand for better support against a very powerful strike. The Number Two Block is used against the Number Two, Four, Seven, and Eleven strikes (backhand strikes and thrusts) of the 12-Strike Sequence.

Number Two Block: Outward.

Number Three Block: Downward Reverse. Sweep the stick downward and inward direction until it is in a diagonal position. This block is specific to the Number Nine Strike of the 12-Strike Sequence. For this block and the next block, you won't be able to brace the stick against a powerful strike, as it would cause you to bend forward, which would leave your face vulnerable to attack. Instead, you can take a step backward momentarily to clear your foot out of the opponent's striking path.

Number Three Block: Downward Reverse.

Number Four Block: Downward.

Number Five Block: Upward.

Number Four Block: Downward. Sweep the stick downward in an outward direction until it is in a diagonal position. This block is specific to the Number Eight Strike of the 12-Strike Sequence. As in the Number Three Block described above, you can take a step backward to clear your foot out of the opponent's striking path.

Number Five Block: Upward. Sweep the stick upward to a horizontal position while bracing it near its pommel with the palm of your second hand. This block is specific to the Number Twelve Strike of the 12-Strike Sequence.

Number Six Block: Vertical. Sweep the stick across the body while keeping it in a vertical position with its tip pointing downward. Brace the stick with the second hand to form a solid frame that will allow you to block hard strikes. This block is specific to the Number Five Strike of the 12-Strike Sequence.

Catching

Catching techniques are checking and grabbing maneuvers that momentarily stall the movement of the opponent's weapon-wielding arm, thereby facilitating a counterattack. In stick combat the check or grab may be directed at either the stick or the arm. In empty-hand combat, it is applied to the arm. In blade combat the check or grab must be placed on

Number Six Block: Vertical.

the arm to prevent your hand from getting cut. Each of the six blocks described above has a basic corresponding catching technique. Students will also learn other catching maneuvers as they advance. Note that although the photos illustrate full grabs, quicker open-hand checks may also be applied to slow down the opponent's movement.

Number One Block and Catch. Block your opponent's forehand strike and catch his stick to prepare for a backhand strike counterattack. This catch corresponds to the Number One Block.

Number Two Block and Catch. Block your opponent's backhand strike and catch his stick to prepare for a forehand strike counterattack. This catch corresponds to the Number Two Block.

Number Three Block and Catch. Block your opponent's downward reverse strike and catch his stick to prepare for a forehand strike counterattack. This catch corresponds to the Number Three Block.

Number Four Block and Catch. Block your opponent's downward strike and catch his stick to prepare for a backhand strike counterattack. This catch corresponds to the Number Four Block.

Number Five Block and Catch. Block your opponent's downward strike and catch his stick to prepare for a downward strike counterattack. This block corresponds to the Number Five Block.

Number Six Block and Catch. Block your opponent's center thrust and catch his stick to prepare for a backhand strike counterattack. This block corresponds to the Number Six Block.

Patterns of Movement

Patterns of movement are combinations of two or more basic striking actions joined together in repetitive sequences. These patterns generally follow geometric patterns such as the X and + shapes, the infinity symbol (∞), or the oval; sometimes, they travel along single horizontal or vertical lines. The initial motion serves as a block or set-up, facilitating the effective delivery of the second and third strikes. The 12-Strike Sequence is the fundamental source for learning several patterns of movement. To identify the various numbered strikes mentioned below (Number One Strike, Number Four Strike, etc.), refer to the section on the 12-Strike Sequence.

Krusada.

Krusada. Start with a Number One Strike and follow up with a Number Two Strike. This completes one cycle and makes an X pattern. Krusada has many applications. You can use it to block against your opponent's weapon and then deliver a counterattack from the opposite direction to his face. Another way to apply this pattern is to strike or cut your opponent's weapon-wielding hand or wrist and follow up with a strike to the face. The initial motion of the pattern can be either forehanded or backhanded. Krusada can be delivered with wide movements or with tighter motions for use in confined areas.

Banda banda.

Banda banda. This pattern uses a side-to-side motion that travels along a horizontal plane. Start with a Number Three Strike and quickly follow up with a Number Four Strike. This completes one cycle. The first movement may be used to strike your opponent's weapon or limb. The second movement attacks the weapon or limb from the opposite angle. When performed in a wide, sweeping manner, banda banda is useful for clearing crowds or for holding a group of assailants at bay. It may also be executed in tighter motions for use in confined spaces.

Sungkiti. Sungkiti (also called *tutsada, tuslok,* or *salag tusok*) represents the deadly thrusting techniques that can devastate an opponent. It is especially effective for combat in places where lateral movement is highly restricted, like tunnels or hallways. Start with a Number Five Strike, follow up with a Number Six Strike, and finish with a Number Seven Strike. Sungkiti aims to attack vulnerable areas like the eyes, throat, solar plexus, underarms, and groin. Although sungkiti can be very effective, one must be careful when applying it, because the technique leaves the attacking limb momentarily extended and vulnerable to counterattacks.

Sungkiti.

Ocho ocho. Ocho ocho means "figure eight," and this pattern of movement follows the path of the infinity symbol (a figure eight turned sideways). Ocho ocho is the reverse of the krusada pattern. Start with a rising forehand strike, and follow up with a rising backhand strike to complete one cycle. Note that these moves do not correspond to specific parts of the 12-Strike Sequence. Ocho ocho may be delivered in a wide or tight manner, depending on the combat situation. The attack travels upward from a low, unexpected angle; it blends well with downward forehand or backhand strikes or with thrusting techniques.

Ocho ocho.

Doblada. This pattern, also known as *doblete,* traces an oval-shaped outline, like a lariat loop. It can be delivered from overhead, it can travel straight downward, or it can travel at a downward, diagonal angle. Doblada has multiple applications and may be utilized at long range to knock an opponent's weapon out of his hands, damaging his weapon-wielding wrist or forearm in the process. A follow-up strike to the head is then possible. Applied in close quarters, doblada is useful for combat in tunnels or hallways where side-to-side movements are difficult to execute. Deliver a Number One Strike and follow through, sweeping the stick across your body. Then, turn your wrist so that your hand is in a palm-down position, loop the stick across the left ear, and deliver another Number One Strike.

Doblada.

Rompida. This pattern uses an up-and-down pattern to trace an imaginary vertical line. It's similar to banda banda, but instead of using a side-to-side movement, rompida moves upward and downward. The first movement is useful for clearing an opponent's weapon out of the way; the second movement follows up to strike a vital area of the body. Rompida may be utilized at long range or—with a slight adjustment to elbow position—at close quarters with equal effectiveness. Deliver a Number Twelve Strike, turn the wrist so that the palm faces to the right, and finish with an upward strike along the same line.

Rompida.

Abaniko.

Abaniko. This pattern follows a fanning motion similar to the unfolding of a Spanish folding fan, hence the name. There are high- and mid-level versions. Abaniko is characterized by a quick turning of the weapon-wielding wrist—often without elbow or forearm movement. Abaniko typically does not have the power to end a confrontation with one hit, but it can be useful for setting up the opponent for the finishing technique. Start in a high forehand position, and hold your stick in a horizontal position above your head as if to deliver a Number Twelve Strike. Without changing positions, snap the stick counterclockwise to strike the opponent's head. Immediately turn the wrist again to deliver another strike, this time going clockwise. The second strike requires that you move your elbow slightly outward to reposition for the strike.

Pilantik.

Pilantik. Pilantik, also called *labtik,* is a quick strike delivered without the wind-up used in many other Kombatan techniques. This is not so much a multi-strike pattern of movement as it is a style of striking, characterized by a snapping motion of the wrist. Pilantik follows a block or deflection or is used to set-up a powerful strike. Several variations of pilantik exist. One of the most common applications starts with the stick on your left side; it should be held in a horizontal position, so that it extends across your body. From this position, you can snap the stick forward to deliver a descending strike to your opponent's weapon-wielding hand; this will often disarm your opponent. You can follow up with a Number Two Strike to the temple.

Pinayong.

Pinayong. Commonly called *hirada bantagueña,* after the Batangas province from which it originated, pinayong is Kombatan's "umbrella" block-and-counter pattern. It consists of an umbrella-like covering block followed by an upward sweeping counter that can impact areas such as the groin, chin, or forearm. The most common variation starts with an upward block against a Number Twelve Strike. Block the downward strike and catch your opponent's stick (grab his wrist if he is holding a blade or other weapon you cannot grab). Sweep your stick backward and downward, and follow through to deliver an upward sweeping strike to the chin.

Pabayo. This group of techniques consists of hammering strikes delivered after a block or deflection with the pommel of the stick. Pabayo got its name from the pestle used by farmers to pound grain. It is mostly used for close-range combat. Common applications of pabayo include strikes delivered à la the Number One, Number Two, Number Three, Number Four, and Number Twelve strikes of the 12-Strike Sequence. Targets include the crown of the head and the temples, jaw, nose, and floating ribs. The most common sequence consists of using a one-two combination following the manner of execution of the krusada pattern.

Pabayo.

An effective stick-fighting guard.

Stick-Fighting Guards

Fighting guards are the postures from which you prepare for and initiate combat. Numerous fighting guards exist, and each has its inherent strengths and weaknesses.

The Kombatan stick-fighting guard is a modified forward stance—the feet are placed slightly closer together than in the standard forward stance. Hold your stick in the forward hand (if the right foot is forward, so is the right hand and vice versa). You want it to be in a diagonal position in front of your body, so that you are effectively placing your weapon between you and your opponent. The second hand is held vertically in front of the chest. This fighting guard allows you to quickly deploy the stick to block or deflect your opponent's strikes or to launch your own offensive maneuvers.

Other fighting guards exist in Kombatan, and they may provide varying degrees of protection and effectiveness for offense measures. Here are the more common ones.

Forehand Strike Guard. This position prepares you to deliver forehand strikes. It's good for executing a strong forehand strike, but it leaves your face and body open to attack.

Backhand Strike Guard. This position prepares you to deliver backhand strikes. It's good for executing a strong backhand strike, but it puts you at risk of having your front arm trapped or hit at the wrist or forearm.

Vertical Strike Guard. This position enables you to deliver downward strikes to the head. It's good for executing a powerful downward strike, but it immediately leaves your face and body open to counterattacks.

Forehand Strike Guard.

Backhand Strike Guard.

Vertical Strike Guard.

An identical technique delivered at long, middle, and short ranges.

Distance and Technique

In arnis distance is viewed as a flowing and dynamic phenomenon. Participants in a real-life combat seldom maintain a neat, controlled distance between them. A fight could start from a distance of eight feet, progress to a closer—and then to an extremely close—range, and return to long range in a matter of seconds. Therefore, you must develop expertise in the varying ranges of combat.

Arnis is unique in that with minor changes, you can adapt each technique to whatever fighting distance you find yourself in. Take the Number Twelve Strike as an example: At a longer range, the practitioner would use a full-arm swing, extending his arm completely to reach his opponent. At medium range, he would simply bend his arm at the elbow to shorten the arc of the swing. At close range, he would keep his elbow close to his body and use hip motion to generate the momentum and power for the swing. Hence, the same technique is applied at three different distances.

Other Stick-Fighting Methods

Paired Weapons: Kombatan also uses paired weapons. One of the most common paired-weapons groupings is the *doble baston* (double cane) method, which consists of two sticks of equal or nearly equal length. The sticks are manipulated in basic patterns that often resemble the *solo baston* method, with the distinction being that the second hand now wields a stick. Using a second stick increases the distance from which you can engage in combat. It also protects the second hand from injury by keeping it farther from the attacker's weapon(s). Some paired-weapons sequences are referred to as *sinawali,* a term denoting a weaving pattern (after the *sawali* weaved mats used as fence material). In the *redonda* pattern, the practitioner twirls the sticks in front of him to form a protective shield.

Another application of paired weapons is the *espada y daga* (literally, "sword and dagger") technique, wherein a long stick and a short stick are used in tandem. The long stick performs techniques similar to those in the *solo baston* method while the short stick thrusts at vital targets on the body. It is said that this technique was adapted from Spanish combat styles.

Doble baston.

Espada y daga.

Stick and chain.

Bangkaw.

For practical purposes, the stick may be paired with nearly any other weapon, including a chain, a folding knife, or a chemical spray like Mace. You can also use any practical object you find lying around the scene of a fight—a bottle, a brick, an ashtray, or a rock—to complement the stick. Remember, in combat you must be prepared to use anything at your disposal in order to survive.

Bangkaw. The *bangkaw* is a six-foot-long staff used to attack and defend from long range. Kombatan features techniques for its use against another staff, as well as against other weapons. A primary advantage of the staff is its extremely long reach. With it, one can counter an attack from an opponent armed with a *bolo* or knife without coming into close proximity. The *bangkaw* is a martial adaptation of the long stick that is used in rural areas of the Philippines to carry two large buckets of water on one shoulder.

Dulo dulo.

Dulo dulo. The *dulo dulo* is a specialty weapon of Kombatan. It is simply a short stick of about six inches, with points at both ends. The *dulo dulo* is used at extremely close quarters to attack sensitive points like the eyes, temples, throat hollow, back of the wrist, sternum, groin, and the mastoid process behind the ear. It can be utilized to strike, to force your opponent to release you from a grabbing attack, or to magnify the effect of a joint lock by attacking the sensitive points you are controlling.

Chapter 9

Blade Combat

The Daga

The Filipino predilection for bladed weapons is evidenced by the wide variety of such implements found throughout the country. These weapons range in length from the nondescript short *daga* to the mid-length *bolo* to the long *kampilan* (popular in the Islamic south). The fighting knife, called *daga,* is also known by the terms *patalim* (meaning "edged weapon") and *panaksak* (meaning "thrusting weapon").

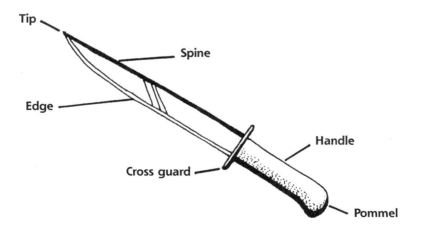

Unlike the stick, the knife can only be held at the handle end to slash, thrust, or deliver pommel blows.

In the 1950s and 1960s knife-fighting was often associated with criminal elements, particularly in Manila. Knives were the weapons commonly favored by street gangs like the Oxo, Sigue Sigue, Sputnik, and the Bahala Na, all of which originated in the tough Manila slum district of Tondo, where a person could get severely beaten or even killed just for being an "outsider." Therefore, it seems natural that the *daga* has been fully incorporated into the Kombatan curriculum.

There is no standard design for the *daga* of Kombatan. It should be noted that while *daga* literally translates as "dagger," a term defined as a "double-edged knife," Kombatan uses the same term to mean any type of knife that can be used for fighting. There are nonetheless some common features that are considered to be ideal for a combat-oriented knife. The first is a sharp blade with a length of approximately seven inches. This ensures practical use in both medium and short ranges. If it were any shorter, it would put you within reach of your opponent's knife. If it were any longer, it would require you to use techniques that would be better served by a *bolo* or machete. Another ideal feature is a cross guard that protects you from having the opponent's knife slide down onto your hand during an exchange. A cross guard also prevents your hand from sliding onto your own blade when you deliver a hard thrusting technique. A third feature is a handle that protrudes far enough from the bottom of your hand to allow for effective pommel blows.

Kombatan practitioners are noted for their ability to utilize any type of knife they can get hold of. By simply being familiar with the specific shape and functions of a particular blade, practitioners can readily make the necessary technical adjustments to employ the blade in combat. The chapter on weapon characteristics includes vital information on the distinct properties associated with various types of blades.

Note that in its given range, the knife is generally a more dangerous weapon than the stick. Whereas the stick requires a certain amount of space to be effective (unless it is used to aid a joint lock or to strangle an opponent), the knife merely needs to touch its target to cause damage. Once the knife has made contact, it can be pulled or pushed to lacerate flesh and bring about serious wounds that can end a confrontation immediately. The effects of a knife attack can vary from a slice *(hiwa)* to a superficial thrust *(sundot)* to a deep, shredding slash *(laslas)* to a chopping and potentially dismembering stroke *(taga)* done with a bigger and heavier knife.

Gripping Fundamentals

You must maintain a proper grip to successfully apply knife techniques. As in its stick-fighting component, Kombatan utilizes a full grip in knife-fighting for stability and power. Wrap your thumb and fingers completely around the knife's handle. Maintain a firm grip, but don't tense the arm and grasp the weapon too tightly. Conversely, do not grasp the knife too loosely, as this will weaken your slashes and thrusts and may cause you to drop your weapon.

Number One Grip. Grip the knife forward, with the blade extending from the thumb side of the hand. Two types of finger positioning are used in the Number One Grip—one with the hand in a standard fist (identical to the grip used in stick-fighting) and one with the index finger and thumb pointing toward the knife's tip. The latter is utilized for straight thrusting attacks. Both grips position the knife so that the cutting edge is facing downward toward the

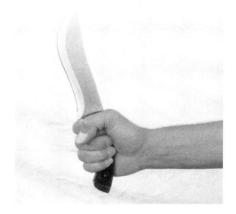

The Number One Grip using the first finger position.

Number Two Grip.

knuckles. In specialized applications, such as sentry-neutralization and close-quarter fighting, the cutting edge may also be held facing upward toward the palm.

Number Two Grip. Hold the knife in the reverse position, with the blade extending from the little-finger side of the hand. Generally, the cutting edge should face downward toward the knuckles, though in specialized applications, the cutting edge may also be held facing upward toward the palm.

Maintaining a proper grip on a knife that doesn't have a cross guard will allow you to deliver powerful thrusts without having to worry that your hand will slide down your own blade in the process. Described

Number One Grip on a knife with no cross guard. Rest the pommel against the side of the little finger.

above are two grips you can use to make knives that don't have cross guards safer to use. Bear in mind that when using a knife with no cross guard, it may be more prudent—and ultimately safer—to deliver slashing maneuvers instead of thrusts, thereby minimizing the likelihood that you'll injure yourself.

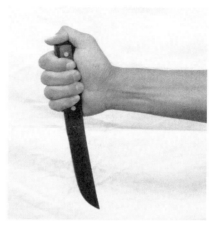

Number Two Grip on a knife with no cross guard. Press the thumb onto the pommel.

Cut hands resulting from using improper grips and knives without cross guards.

An identical technique delivered at long, middle, and short ranges.

Like stick techniques, knife techniques may be used at long, medium, or short ranges. A long slash utilizes the entire length of the arm. A medium slash requires you to bend your arm at the elbow to shorten your reach. A short slash requires you to keep your elbow close to your body and use your hip motion to generate power. In this way, the same maneuver can be applied in all situations by making slight adjustments.

Slashes, Thrusts, and Pommel Blows

With the knife held in the Number One Grip you can execute the 12-Strike Sequence as it described in the section on stick-fighting. The krusada, banda banda, sungkiti, ocho ocho, doblada, rompida, pinayong, and pabayo patterns of movement may also be practiced using the Number One Grip—another direct translation of the techniques from stick-fighting to knife-fighting.

Delivering the 12-Strike Sequence with the knife held in the Number Two Grip transforms the slashing techniques into thrusting techniques and the thrusting techniques into slashing techniques. Therefore, regardless of the grip used, the knife can be used to effectively implement the sequence.

Slashing *(laslas)*, thrusting *(saksak)*, and striking with the pommel *(bayo)* are the three main operations performed with the knife. As in stick work, each type of technique may be delivered along the horizontal, vertical, and diagonal lines of the Universal Angles of Motion pattern. The primary knife techniques of Kombatan are listed below.

Forehand Diagonal Slash. Start in a high forehand position, and slash inward along a downward diagonal angle. Targets include the face, neck, forearms, wrists, hands, and knees.

Forehand Diagonal Slash.

Forehand Diagonal Thrust. Start in a high forehand position, and thrust inward along a downward diagonal angle. Targets include the eyes and the throat.

Forehand Diagonal Pommel. Start in a high forehand position, and strike inward along a downward diagonal angle using the pommel of the knife. Targets include the temples, nose, and jaw.

Forehand Diagonal Thrust (Number Two Grip). Start in a high forehand position, and thrust inward along a downward diagonal angle. Targets include the eyes and the neck.

Backhand Diagonal Slash. Start in a high backhand position, and slash outward along a downward diagonal angle. Targets include the face, neck, forearm, wrists, hands, and knees.

Backhand Diagonal Thrust. Start in a high backhand position, and thrust outward along a downward diagonal angle. Targets include the eyes and the throat.

Backhand Diagonal Pommel. Start in a high backhand position, and strike outward along a downward diagonal angle using the pommel of the knife. Targets include the temples, nose, and jaw.

Forehand Diagonal Thrust.

Forehand Diagonal Thrust (Number Two Grip).

Forehand Diagonal Thrust (Number Two Grip).

Backhand Diagonal Slash.

Backhand Diagonal Thrust.

Backhand Diagonal Pommel.

Backhand Diagonal Thrust (Number Two Grip). Start in a high forehand position, and thrust outward along a downward diagonal angle. Targets include the eyes and the neck.

Forehand Horizontal Slash. Start in a middle forehand position, and slash inward along a horizontal angle. Targets include the throat, abdominal region, forearms, wrists, hands, and (if you are kneeling) the knees and shins.

Forehand Horizontal Thrust. Start in a middle forehand position, and thrust inward at a horizontal angle. Targets include the throat, eyes, underarms, abdomen, and groin.

Forehand Horizontal Pommel. Start in a middle forehand position, and strike inward at a horizontal angle using the pommel of the knife. Targets include the jaw and floating ribs.

Forehand Horizontal Slash (Number Two Grip). Start in a middle forehand position, and slash inward along a horizontal angle. Targets include the throat, abdomen, forearms, wrists, hands, and (if you are kneeling) the knees and shins.

Forehand Horizontal Thrust (Number Two Grip). Start in a middle forehand position, and thrust inward at a horizontal angle. Targets include the throat, eyes, underarms, abdomen, and groin.

Backhand Diagonal Thrust (Number Two Grip).

Forehand Horizontal Slash.

Forehand Horizontal Thrust.

Forehand Horizontal Pommel.

Forehand Horizontal Slash (Number Two Grip).

Forehand Horizontal Thrust (Number Two Grip).

Backhand Horizontal Slash. Start in a middle backhand position, and slash outward along a horizontal angle. Targets include the throat, abdomen, forearms, wrists, hands, and (if you are kneeling) the knees and shins.

Backhand Horizontal Thrust. Start in a middle backhand position, and thrust outward at a horizontal angle. Targets include the throat, eyes, underarms, abdomen, and groin.

Backhand Horizontal Pommel. Start in a middle backhand position, and strike outward at a horizontal angle using the pommel of the stick. Targets include the throat, jaw, and floating ribs.

Backhand Horizontal Slash (Number Two Grip). Start in a middle backhand position, and slash outward along a horizontal angle. Targets include the throat, abdominal region, forearms, wrists, hands, and (if you are kneeling) the knees and shins.

Backhand Horizontal Thrust (Number Two Grip). Start in a middle backhand position, and thrust outward at a horizontal angle. Targets include the neck, eyes, underarms, abdomen, and groin.

Forward Thrust. Hold the knife close to the right hip and deliver a straight thrust. Targets include the throat, underarms, and midsection.

Backhand Horizontal Slash.

Backhand Horizontal Thrust.

Backhand Horizontal Pommel.

Backhand Horizontal Slash (Number Two Grip).

Backhand Horizontal Thrust (Number Two Grip).

Forward Thrust.

Forward Slash (Number Two Grip). Deliver a rising center slash (the slash should follow a vertical path). Targets include the groin, forearms, wrists, hands, and chin.

Downward Slash. Start in a high forehand position, and deliver a downward slash. Targets include the forehead, forearms, wrists, hands, and (on an opponent who is bending forward) the nape of the neck.

Downward Pommel. Start in a high forehand position, and deliver a downward strike using the pommel of the knife. Targets include the crown of the head; the forearms, wrists, and hands; and (on an opponent who is bending forward) the nape of the neck.

Downward Thrust (Number Two Grip). Start in a high forehand position, and deliver a downward thrust. Targets include the eyes and the shoulder well below the clavicle (this attacks the subclavian artery; it's a common sentry-neutralization technique).

Forward Slash (Number Two Grip).

Downward Slash.

Downward Pommel.

Downward Thrust (Number Two Grip).

Blocks and Deflections

With the exception of the Number Six Block, the blocks and deflections used in knife-fighting closely resemble those used in stick-fighting; however, in knife-fighting, blocks and deflections are actually slashes that can instantly disable the opponent's weapon-wielding limb by attacking the forearm, wrist, or hand.

Number One Block (Inward). Sweep the knife inward, slashing your opponent's attacking arm. This block is used against forehand slashes and thrusts above the waist.

Number Two Block (Outward). Sweep the knife outward, slashing your opponent's attacking arm. This block is used against backhand slashes and thrusts above the waist.

Number Three Block (Downward Reverse). Sweep the knife downward and inward, slashing your opponent's attacking arm. This block is a specific counter against a low forehand slash aimed at targets below the waist.

Number Four Block (Downward). Sweep the knife downward and outward, slashing your opponent's attacking arm. This block is a specific counter against a low backhand slash aimed at targets below the waist.

Number Five Block (Upward). Sweep the knife upward and outward, slashing your opponent's attacking arm. This block counters an overhand slash or—when your opponent uses the Number Two Grip—a stabbing attack.

Number Six Block (Downward Horizontal). Sweep the knife downward, slashing your opponent's attacking arm. This block counters a center thrust aimed at the abdomen or groin.

Number One Block (Inward).

Number Two Block (Outward).

Number Three Block (Downward Reverse).

Number Four Block (Downward).

Number Five Block (Upward).

Number Six Block (Downward Horizontal).

Knife-Fighting Guards

You can place the knife in either hand. A crucial part of good knife-fighting form is to keep your knife-wielding hand in motion to prevent it from being struck. Avoid unnecessarily elaborate movements, however, as these may serve merely to foil your own offensive efforts. What's more, a skilled opponent can immediately sense an overly fancy pattern of movement and stage an instant attack of his own.

Typical knife-fighting guards.

From Defense to Offense: Combat Applications

Using six basic knife attacks, we can illustrate a number of possible blocks and counters.

Opponent attacks with an inward slash. Block inward—slashing your opponent's forearm in the process—and grab the wrist. Counter with a slash to the torso—drag the knife outward. As soon as you withdraw your knife from this counter, deliver a strong forward thrust to the abdomen. Be sure to maintain a solid grip on your knife when doing thrusting maneuvers.

Countering an inward slash.

Opponent attacks with an outward slash. Block outward—slashing your opponent's wrist in the process—and grab the forearm. Withdraw your knife and deliver a counterthrust to the abdomen.

Countering an outward slash.

Opponent attacks with a low inward slash. Block inward—slashing your opponent's forearm in the process—and grab the wrist to immobilize it momentarily. Withdraw your knife and deliver an outward slash to the eye.

Countering a low inward slash.

Opponent attacks with a low outward slash. Block outward—slashing your opponent's forearm in the process—and grab the wrist to immobilize it. Withdraw your knife and deliver an inward slash to the eye.

Countering a low outward slash.

Opponent attacks with a descending slash. Block upward—slashing your opponent's forearm in the process—and grab the wrist. Withdraw your knife and deliver an inward slash to the eye. Follow up with a penetrating upward thrust to the throat.

Countering a descending slash.

Opponent attacks with a low, gutting thrust. Block downward—slashing your opponent's forearm in the process—and check the wrist. After you've checked the wrist, grab it, and deliver a thrust to the eye. (Note that for safety reasons, the knife's point is shown traveling past the eye in the above photo).

Countering a low, gutting thrust.

Other Blade Methods

Bolos. The *bolo,* also called the *itak,* is the general utility blade of the Filipino farmer. It usually ranges from fourteen to twenty-four inches in length, though some blades are even longer. Although Kombatan techniques are commonly practiced with the *bolo,* they are equally effective when practiced with other blades of similar lengths, such as the *binakoko,* which was patterned after a type of fish; the *dinahong palay,* the design of which was inspired by a poisonous snake; the *barang,* which is a flat-headed chopper; or the *kris* and *kampilan,* two swords commonly used in the southern provinces.

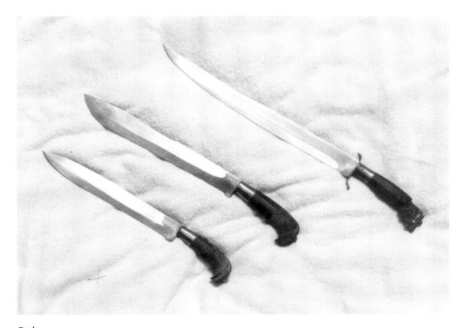

Bolos.

Balisong. The *balisong,* a fan knife that has gained some popularity in the West, was invented in the 1940s in the Tagalog province of Batangas by Perfecto de Leon. One curious account depicts the visionary de Leon as a simple man married to an overbearing wife. One day, after being berated by his wife for accidentally breaking a knife blade while trying to complete a chore, the dejected de Leon retired to his favorite resting place on a riverbank. While trying to cool himself from the intense tropical heat with an *abaniko,* or folding fan, de Leon came up with the idea of encasing a knife blade in two pieces of wood and metal that would be connected by a hinge at the base. The wooden pieces would then effectively serve as a built-in scabbard. The knife could be opened and closed using a simple flicking motion of the wrist, similar to the action of opening and closing a fan. Increasingly complex opening and closing techniques have evolved in knife circles since the *balisong*'s invention. This type of knife has been incorporated into the arsenal of Kombatan and many other Filipino martial arts systems.

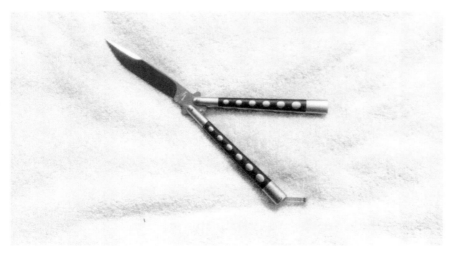

Balisong.

Chapter 10

Empty-Hand Combat

Mano Mano: The Final Option

Empty-hand combat is taught after students achieve basic proficiency in the use of weaponry. This does not mean that bare-handed skills are considered to be of any lesser or greater value than weapons skills. By placing weapons-training first arnis instructors are simply following the fundamental rule that an opponent may arm himself when engaging in combat. The importance placed on weapons training also observes the basic fact that knowing how to use a weapon gives you a decided advantage in any given confrontation.

Unlike a sports match, which pits con-testants one-on-one based on their physical dimensions and dictates that they use identical techniques and weapons, street combat is never an equal situation, and it involves many elements of uncertainty. You might have to face a larger opponent. You might come up against an assailant armed with a knife or club. You might be jumped by a group of attackers.

And the confrontation could take place anywhere from a deserted parking lot to a crowded restaurant to a dark hallway.

Empty-hand combat skills are nonetheless very important. You may find yourself in a setting where it is not practical or even legal to bear weapons, such as a beach, an airport, a courthouse, a school facility, or a government building. The only option then is to fight empty-handed. This is where *mano mano* (from the Spanish term *mano a mano,* meaning "hand-to-hand") and *buno* (native wrestling) come in.

Mano mano consists of hand and foot techniques, which are delivered to vulnerable points on an opponent's body. The hands are the body's primary weapons—they are versatile and can be readily employed in rapid sequences. The basic hand formations are the fist, the spear hand, and the palm heel. The elbow is classified as a hand technique by default, as it is delivered with the arms rather than the legs.

Important: Unless otherwise noted, the striking and grappling techniques described below all use what we refer to as a "ready guard." This guard is a modified forward stance—your feet should be slightly closer together than in a standard forward stance. Hold your hands in front of your body to protect your face and torso; this posture is similar in style to a Western-style boxing guard.

Hand Techniques

Straight Punch. The straight punch is delivered to the nose, temples, jaw, chin, abdomen, or floating ribs. Start in a ready guard, and project the right fist forward explosively. Exhale as you throw the punch to generate more power and tense your body at the moment of impact.

Straight Punch.

Spear Hand. The spear hand uses the tips of the outstretched fingers to attack softer spots on the opponent's body, such as the eyes and the throat. Start in a ready guard, and without drawing the hand back to telegraph your movement, quickly extend the open hand, and strike the target. The spear hand is especially effective in executing quick flurries of strikes without having to retract the arm too far back.

Spear Hand.

Straight Palm Strike. The straight palm strike is used to attack the nose, chin, jaw, and ribs. If applied properly, it poses fewer risks of breaking your hand, which is a real possibility when making impact with a hard surface such as the chin. Start in a ready guard, and using a straight punch motion, make contact with the heel of the palm instead of the fist.

Straight Palm Strike.

Front Elbow Strike.

Front Elbow Strike. This is a powerful application of the elbow. Start in a ready guard, and deliver the elbow forward horizontally (so that it's parallel to the ground, with your knuckles facing upward and your hand open). Use it to strike the temple, nose, jaw, or chin. A versatile weapon, the elbow can also strike upward, sideways, or downward (to the head of an opponent who is bending forward).

Foot Techniques

The feet and legs are important long-range weapons that can often deliver stronger blows than the hands. Because modern-day garb typically includes some sort of footwear, kicking techniques are also safer than punching techniques, because hard shoes—instead of the small bones of the hands—are used to strike unprotected areas of an opponent's body.

For all of the techniques listed below your starting position should be the same ready guard used for punching techniques.

Front Kick.

Front Kick. Start in a ready guard. Raise your right knee above your belt, and extend the leg forward in an explosive manner, using the ball of the foot to attack the abdomen, ribs, chin, jaw, or nose. After kicking, retract the leg back toward your body before lowering it.

Side Kick. Start in a ready guard, and cross your right leg behind your left leg, so that you are standing sideways to your opponent. Raise your left knee above your belt and extend the leg sideways in an explosive manner. The toes of the support leg should face in the direction opposite the kick for maximum power and extension. The kick is aimed at the abdomen, ribs, chest, chin, jaw, nose, or temple. Retract the kicking leg back toward your body before lowering it.

Side Kick.

Knee Strike. Start in a ready guard. Raise the knee upward and forward in one smooth motion, spearing the target (groin, abdomen, or ribs) with the tip. To generate more power, make a pulling motion with your hands as you knee. You can deliver a knee strike to an opponent's face, but this move requires you to grab the back of his or her head and pull it down into the strike.

Knee Strike.

Roundhouse Kick. Start in a ready guard. Raise your right knee to the side, and with a twist of the hips, deliver the kick in a circular motion to the target. The support foot pivots as the kick is extended so that the toes are pointing in the direction opposite to the kick. The targets are the groin, ribs, abdomen, throat, chin, jaw, nose, or tem-

Roundhouse Kick.

ples. Delivered correctly, the roundhouse kick is a devastating technique that can produce a knockout or broken bones. Note that the technique for the left roundhouse kick varies slightly—for the purposes of this book, only the more powerful rear leg kick has been illustrated.

Grappling Techniques

Buno consists of throws and grappling techniques applied at close range. As most fights eventually brings you into close proximity with your opponent, opportunities to apply *buno* techniques commonly arise.

Outside Sweep.

Outside Sweep. The outside sweep is a basic takedown that has many uses and can be applied from different positions. Start in a ready guard. Block your opponent's hooking punch (an arcing fist strike that travels from the outside in) with your left hand. Grab his arm and counter immediately with a straight right punch to his face, which will force his weight to shift to the rear. Quickly step in with the left foot, driving it past his right foot, and sweep your right calf against his right calf to knock him to the ground. Follow up with a descending punch or a kick. A descending punch is delivered exactly as a straight punch, but in a downward motion. Alternatively, a low side kick can be delivered in a downward motion on a fallen opponent.

Foot Hook. The front hook is a powerful takedown that attacks the opponent's ankle. It can be applied after you have blocked your opponent's punch and grabbed his arm for control. From a right-foot-forward stance, sweep the left foot along the ground and strike his ankle from the back to knock him to the ground. Follow up with a descending punch or kick. For further follow-up, a joint-locking or strangulation technique is also possible.

Armbar Takedown. The armbar takedown can be applied whenever your opponent's arm is in an extended position. If your opponent attempts a right backhanded blow (with or without a weapon), block it outward with your right hand, grab his wrist, and brace the blade of your left forearm against his elbow joint. While exerting pressure on the elbow, wheel him around clockwise and force him into a facedown position on the ground. You can then hold your opponent in place by kneeling on his elbow; this allows you to deliver follow-up striking techniques. Instead of completing the takedown, you may choose to simply break the elbow by smashing it with your forearm.

Front Trip. The front trip is an extension of the armbar takedown. If your opponent resists your initial takedown attempt, sweep your left foot backward, impacting the front

Foot Hook.

Armbar Takedown.

Front Trip.

of his knee to take him to the ground. A follow-up as described in the armbar technique is then possible.

Inward Block.

Outward Block.

Blocks and Deflections
Against an Empty-Handed Opponent

Inward Block. Sweep your arm across your body, blocking your opponent's attack with your forearm or palm. The inward block is effective against straight or hooking hand strikes or against high kicks. A catching technique can follow this block, allowing you to control your opponent's limb and begin your counterattack.

Outward Block. Sweep your arm outward, blocking your opponent's attack with your forearm. The outward block is effective against straight or hooking hand strikes or against high kicks. A catching technique can follow this block, allowing you to control your opponent's limb and begin your counterattack.

Reverse Block. Sweep your arm inward at a low angle, blocking your opponent's hand or foot strike with your forearm. The reverse block is effective against straight or hooking strikes aimed at mid- and low-level targets. A catching technique can follow this block, allowing you to control your opponent's limb and begin your counterattack.

Reverse Block.

Downward Block. Sweep your arm downward at a low angle, blocking your opponent's hand or foot strike with your forearm. The downward block is effective against straight or hooking strikes aimed at mid- and low-level targets. A catching technique can follow this block, allowing you to control your opponent's limb and begin your counterattack

Downward Block.

Upward Block. Raise your forearm to block a high-level strike. The upward block is effective against strikes that come at a descending angle from above. A catching technique can follow this block, allowing you to control your opponent's limb and begin your counterattack.

Upward Block.

Against an Armed Opponent

Blocking attacks from an opponent armed with a club-type or edged weapon requires a modified set of movements. Below are blocks against four basic attacks.

An inward block against a knife attack.

Inward Block. Block your opponent's right inward slash (or thrust) with the edge of the left hand and the right forearm. The left hand catches your opponent's wrist, allowing you to execute a counterattack—you can throw a punch to his face with your right hand and follow up with an outside sweep to take him to the ground, where you can disarm him.

An outward block against a knife attack.

Outward Block. Block your opponent's right outward slash (or reverse thrust) with the your right hand and left forearm. The right hand catches your opponent's wrist, allowing you to deliver a counterattack—you can throw a punch to his face with your left hand and follow up with an armbar takedown. Once your opponent's on the ground you can disarm him or hit him with descending strikes.

Downward Block. Block your opponent's right upward and forward thrusting attack by putting your left palm on his wrist and your right forearm against his forearm. The left hand catches the wrist, allowing you to deliver a knee strike and an outside sweep, which will take your opponent to the ground, where you can disarm him. To use this block against a stick attack, you will need to sidestep slightly before executing the block.

A downward block against a knife attack.

Upward Block. Block your opponent's right downward slash (or thrust) with your right hand and left forearm. To do this move correctly, you must step into the strike before it descends completely. The right hand catches the wrist, allowing you to lever your left forearm against the opponent's elbow joint and twist his arm clockwise into an armbar takedown.

An upward block against a knife attack.

Chapter 11

Preparing for Battle

Simply knowing how to execute the various Kombatan techniques does not ensure survival during a violent encounter. Several other key components must be developed to realistically expect success in the turbulent arena of real-life combat. These components are a) physical conditioning, b) technical proficiency, and c) combat readiness.

Physical Conditioning

Fitness is of vital importance to arnis training. You may face a strong, tough fighter who does not immediately succumb to your offensive maneuvers. You may need to wear him down incrementally. Sustaining a fight for the time it would take to do this requires a certain level of fitness.

Kombatan fitness consists of three areas of development: flexibility, strength, and endurance. Flexibility allows you to deliver the various techniques without suffering pulled muscles or torn ligaments. It ensures that you have maximum range of motion for your offensive and defensive techniques, which allows you to fight effectively from any distance.

To increase flexibility, execute side twists, side bends, front bends, back bends, and rotations of the neck and upper body. From a forward stance, lift the straight back leg forward and upward, gradually increasing the height of the foot. Stand with your legs parallel and shoulder-width apart, and lift each leg to the side in a side kick position. Sit on the ground, bend forward from the waist, and gradually attempt to touch your toes. Lie on the ground and keeping your legs joined together and straight, try to touch your toes to the ground by lifting your legs over your head. Remember to relax while doing these stretches, and do not force any of the movements.

Strength *(lakas)* imparts authority to your movements. A weak technique is virtually useless against an opponent who is intent on doing you harm. By developing and maintaining strength, you will develop a natural physical advantage over a weaker opponent and will better able to stand up to a stronger opponent.

Building up strength does not require elaborate equipment or facilities. A set of free weights (barbells and dumbbells) will suffice, providing you use it consistently. You need to practice calisthenics regularly, too. These include essential exercises like sit-ups, free squats, leg-raises, and push-ups. Pull-ups on a horizontal bar, if you have one available, also increase upper body strength. Using a barbell or dumbbells, execute curls, standing presses, and floor or bench presses. Any book on basic weight training will illustrate these and other weight-based exercises.

Finally, endurance enables you to engage in combat for extended periods of time. By exhausting a determined assailant, you improve your chances of prevailing in a fight. Run and skip rope regularly to develop your stamina.

Technical Proficiency

The speed and quality of a practitioner's movements indicate his skill *(galing)* level. By training properly, you can become proficient in stick, blade, and empty-hand combat.

Kombatan uses drills to train students to react instinctively to an attack. Once these drills are absorbed, practitioners test their techniques through sparring sessions, both controlled and unrehearsed. Controlled sparring limits the types of techniques both students can employ. Unrehearsed sparring, as the term suggests, allows both partners to apply their skills in a free and unrestrained way. This freedom, however, does not mean that you are allowed to injure or incapacitate your training partner. You should deliver your techniques purposefully, while still exercising enough control to prevent causing serious injuries. With mutual improvement as your shared goal, you and your training partner should be able to exchange maneuvers and effectively hone your fluency, power, speed, and timing. Sparring like this will also help to identify the methods that work best for you.

Below is a brief rundown of vital Kombatan training drills.

Solo Practice

Air Striking. In this exercise, students execute stick, blade, and empty-handed strikes and defensive maneuvers in the air. This practice is fundamental to learning the techniques and developing precision, and it

Solo practice using long and short sticks and a dagger.

will eventually lead to effective application of the techniques. You can stay in a fixed stance and practice ten repetitions of each movement or you can move from stance to stance as you execute the maneuvers. You can also practice with paired weapons such as double sticks, long and short blades, and stick-and-dagger combinations.

Note that in the early stages of training, you may develop a blister below the base of your index finger from repetitive friction with the stick. This should disappear in time—just be sure not to aggravate it by insisting on hard training in spite of the blister.

Heavybag Drills. You can practice hand and foot strikes on a punching bag. This produces essentially the same effect as training on striking pads (see below), the difference being that on a heavybag, you can deliver full-power blows that may overwhelm a weaker training partner during pad work.

Tire Striking. Hang an old tire from a tree and practice strikes, thrusts, and pommel blows on it using a stick. This is a good exercise for developing a feel for hitting solid surfaces. It complements the air-striking drills well.

Partner Drills

Stick-to-Target Orientation. When a partner is available, you can practice the same strikes and combinations you practiced in the air or on the heavybag. The added benefit here is that you get to place the maneuvers on actual targets, which helps develop precision and the ability to judge distances. Just make sure to control your movements and proceed slowly, so that you don't injure your training partner. You may also practice with other weapons that you may end up using in a fight, like a length of rubber hose, a metal pipe, or telescopic baton.

Practice slashing, thrusting, and pommel blows on a training partner. Don't forget to practice with other weapons, like the telescopic baton shown here.

Knife-Edge Orientation. Practice various slashes, thrusts, and pommel blows on a training partner. You can use rubber or wooden knives at first and progress to live blades. Obviously, you must exercise caution when practicing with real blades.

Partner Strikes and Blocks (Sticks). Practice striking and blocking techniques with a partner. You may deliver a strike, thrust, or pommel blow, to which your partner responds by executing the proper block. Take turns attacking and defending. Slowly increase the power and speed of the strikes to simulate real fighting.

Partner Strikes and Blocks (Knives). Practice striking and blocking with a partner. You may deliver a slash, thrust, or pommel blow, to which your partner responds by executing the proper block and counterattacking. Take turns attacking and defending.

Partner Strikes and Blocks (Empty Hands). Practice striking and blocking using empty-hand techniques. You may deliver a punch, strike, or kick, to which your partner responds by executing a blocking technique. Take turns attacking and defending. Start out slowly and do not use full power.

Pad Work. You and your partner can practice empty-hand techniques using special pads. Deliver hand and foot strikes to striking pads held by your training partner. Pad work is important because it helps you develop a feel for hitting a solid target while it builds your strength and power. The pad-holder can also move around, which helps you learn how to make adjustments for combat at different distances.

Empty-hand Defense Against Weapons. Practice defending against and countering an armed attack. For knife combat, start by working with wooden knives and *bolos,* and progress to working with live blades. Exercise extreme caution when training with real blades.

Sparring

Sparring with Padded Sticks. Today, especially in the West, you can engage in free sparring using foam-padded sticks of equal length to your actual sticks. Because of the safety these sticks provide, you can go at a relatively fast pace, which develops your reflexes and your ability to deal with rapid attacks.

Sparring with Live Sticks. When you use rattan or hardwood sticks, you must spar at a slower pace. This type of sparring requires greater control and must be practiced carefully. As you will discover, even a hit with a small, thin stick can produce significant pain and/or injury when impact is made to bony surfaces like the fingers, wrists, and elbows.

Empty-handed practice against the knife.

Sparring with live sticks. Make sure to control your power to avoid injuring your partner.

Sparring with Wooden Knives. You can also engage in free sparring using wooden knives. Although wood does not have the same ability as metal to damage a target, practicing with wooden knives will give you a general feel for manipulating a bladed weapon.

Combat Readiness

Put together, the above-mentioned drills and exercises cultivate the necessary mental aspects of arnis combat: courage *(lakas loob)* and presence of mind *(pagka-alisto)*. A basic principle urges the Kombatan practitioner to treat his martial arts training with utmost seriousness: He regards training as actual fighting and fighting as a natural extension and application of his training.

Realizing that one cannot realistically account for all possibilities in combat, there is also an age-old Filipino saying "Bahala na," which loosely translates as "Come what may." This can be viewed simply as a fatalistic outlook or as an act of surrendering of the outcome of a given conflict to God *(Bahala na ang Diyos)*.

Chapter 12

Weapon Characteristics

In real-life combat, you can expect to deal with a variety of weapons, some of which you may not have encountered before. These could include club-type, bladed, flexible, projectile, composite, or improvised implements. By virtue of his or her training, the arnis practitioner should have the ability to counter any kind of attack he or she might face. This ability requires a fundamental understanding of the properties of each type of weapon. The critical factor in countering a weapon attack is realizing the danger a specific weapon type poses and the damage it may cause. Below, we'll take a look at the crucial elements to consider when assessing an opponent's weapon.

Some of the weapons you might encounter in a confrontation. Don't be disturbed by a bizarre or unusual-looking weapon. If you concentrate on a weapon's design and stick to basics, you should be able to counter it effectively.

Weapon Length. A staff or spear has a long reach and can cause damage from a distance. It has less utility, however, at close range. Conversely, a knife is dangerous in close quarters, but to use it your opponent must step in to reach you, especially if the conflict starts at a distance.

Weapon Design/Shape. A weapon can be straight, hooked, curved, or have an irregular shape. A sickle with a concave blade can hook around a block or guard, as can a meat hook. A *kukri,* also with a concave blade, cuts with the tip first and can curve around a block or guard. A scimitar with a convex blade cuts with the middle portion first and requires that the opponent be relatively close to be effective. An ax hits with the ax head first, as does a shovel. A *bolo* or machete is dangerous at the edge and tip and (in close quarters) the pommel. An ice pick has no cutting edge but the tip and is therefore used for thrusting attacks. A full *tang* (a fixed-blade knife) is almost always structurally stronger than a folding knife—the metal extends all the way to the pommel, making the knife one solid piece. A folding knife, on the other hand, is in essence already "broken" and is held together at a joint by a pin.

Weapon Material. A weapon can be made of solid metal, chain, wood, rubber, plastic, glass, or a composite material. A solid metal bar is the sturdiest among this group. A chain can wrap around a guard and strike its target, but it's generally only good for a single strike and is most effective in a surprise attack. A hybrid weapon like the nunchaku combines the features of a flexible weapon with an impact weapon. Wood is sturdy but can break with sufficient pressure. Rubber imparts a different, rebounding type of impact. Plastics or thin woods are generally impractical for clubbing blows but can still be useful for thrusting strikes to vital targets.

Weapon Weight and Density. Heavier weapons are capable of powerful but slow clubbing blows. These are best employed when there is adequate time in between to reload for each strike. Lighter sticks can strike multiple times in rapid succession with less wind-up.

Weapon Grip. How the opponent holds his or her weapon also affects its use. A forward or reverse grip on a knife, for example, alters its range and cutting capabilities. Keep in mind that the opponent may also change grips in the middle of the confrontation.

Weapon Versatility. Some weapons have multiple potential uses. A brick is dangerous up close as an impact weapon or at longer distances as a projectile. A nunchaku, made up of two sticks joined by a rope or chain, is a hybrid weapon that combines properties of both impact and flexible weapons.

Other Factors

Place of Conflict. The location of an encounter also dictates whether a weapon will be effective. A conflict could occur in a small space like a telephone booth, where a lead pipe would obviously be impractical. In a large space like a ball field, a knife is at a disadvantage against a long pole. Fighting in a cluttered room or a tunnel-like hallway adversely affects the delivery of most swinging stick-fighting strikes. In addition, you may have to contend with flooring or ground that's slippery, muddy, rough, or uneven. Foliage or branches could also pose obstacles, altering weapon strategies and techniques.

Visibility. Fighting in low light changes the way you would counter a weapon technique, as does the position of a strong light source like the sun. In limited light, you are forced to rely more on feel and instinct than sight. When fighting outdoors, you should try to make your opponent face the sun to impair his or her vision.

Awareness. Finally, your ability to perceive an attack without being caught off-guard must be taken into consideration. A surprise attack that goes unseen until it is near completion is probably the worst-case scenario. Facing a skilled opponent who knows what target to strike makes a difficult fight even worse. In the section on self-defense, we will examine the measures you can take to prevent being caught off-guard by would-be attackers.

With all of these variables in play, students often ask, "What is the best weapon?" The answer is simply: It depends on the particular situation and on the person utilizing the weapon.

Stick, Blade, or Empty Hand?

Opposite is a comparison of the strong and weak points inherent in each of the three main Kombatan weapons.

In summary, the stick has a natural advantage at longer ranges because of its reach. If a fight occurs at medium range, the stick is still the most effective weapon because with it one can reach the opponent's weapon-holding hand without coming into close contact. At close range, the stick may still be used, particularly if the practitioner can angle away from his or her opponent. At extremely close range, however, it is difficult to generate the necessary momentum for a powerful stick strike; therefore, the knife and empty hands, in that order, would be better options.

STICK	BLADE	EMPTY HAND
LEGALITY	LEGALITY	LEGALITY
May be illegal to carry in some places.	May be illegal to carry in some places.	Always available.
EFFECTIVENESS	EFFECTIVENESS	EFFECTIVENESS
Effective versus other sticks, blades, or empty-hand techniques.	Effective versus other knives and empty-hand techniques. Possibly effective against sticks.	Effective versus empty-hand techniques. Puts you at a disadvantage versus sticks or knives.
DURABILITY	DURABILITY	DURABILITY
Resistant to breakage.	Resistant to breakage.	Subject to structural damage and injury.
CONCEALABILITY	CONCEALABILITY	CONCEALABILITY
Highly evident and difficult to conceal.	May be concealed in shirt, jacket, or pants.	Not detectable as an obvious weapon.
STABILITY	STABILITY	STABILITY
May be dropped or knocked out of your hand.	May be dropped or knocked out of your hand.	Reliable and stable unless you are injured.

Chapter 13

Self-Defense: A Matter of Survival

Self-defense in the real world consists of more than just learning and mastering a set of combative maneuvers. It also includes important factors like awareness, prevention, information-gathering, consistent training, and skill maintenance. The first three factors are more universal in nature and must be practiced constantly and with great diligence.

A vital survival principle in Filipino martial arts states, "Maging laging handa," or "Always be prepared." You must be ready to engage in conflict at all times. This is not meant to urge paranoia, but it does compel the practitioner to maintain a constant sharp awareness of his or her surroundings, enabling him or her to identify a potential threat or perceive the first moments of an attack. Constant awareness will prevent you from falling victim to an ambush. Remember that an attack could conceivably come at any time of the day and could come from a total stranger, an acquaintance, or even a relative.

Prepare for the unexpected. It is a fundamental truth in combat that there is no defense against a surprise attack. While it is possible to recover from a surprise attack, the best remedy against one is to stay aware and to take preventative measures. "Maging laging handa" is especially important against the cowardly sneak attack or sucker punch (pa-traidor).

The areas of prevention and information-gathering require you to pay close attention to trends in your community and beyond. Know the trouble spots around you. Although most people don't equate reading and listening to the news with self-defense, consider the following scenario: A news item describes how an armed individual has been holding up pedestrians in a given part of town. Knowing the criminal's description and his general area of operation will keep you on your guard when traveling in that vicinity, which will make it more difficult for you to be victimized. If possible, stay away from neighborhoods with a distinct reputation for drug dealing, gang activity, and general criminal elements. Exercising this piece of common sense could save your life.

Circumstances may sometimes demand that you travel to unfamiliar or undesirable areas. Some basic measures can significantly improve your chances of survival. Keep your automobile in good running condition. Keep at least a half-tank of gas in it at all times. This prevents you from breaking down or running out of fuel, leaving you stranded in unfamiliar or hostile territory. Know where you are going, either with maps or directions from the person you are seeing. At street intersections, always leave some room to maneuver—don't let yourself get boxed in.

When walking, stay in well-lit and well-traveled areas. Avoid bushes and blind corners. Cross the street away from a suspicious-looking figure coming your way. Watch out for the stranger who tries to get too friendly—he could be trying to get you to relax so that he may catch you off-guard. Beware the occupied, parked car with its engine running—it may be a set-up for abduction.

Keep your doors and windows locked, including those above the ground floor. It can be surprising what a determined criminal will do to get to his target. If you keep weapons in the house, keep them in strategic places, so that they are out of sight but easily accessible to you in case of an emergency.

Be especially careful to whom you give out personal information. With advances in modern technology, it is extremely difficult to maintain privacy. Nonetheless, make it harder for the would-be attacker to obtain your information, which could be used to victimize you.

Of course, consistent training and skill maintenance play vital roles in effective self-defense. These we have already touched upon in the section entitled Preparing for Battle.

When physical conflict actually arises, there are two essential principles to observe:

Huwag kang magpapauna. "Don't let the opponent get the jump on you." Act promptly once you perceive a threat. Hesitating in the face of real danger leaves the advantage in the hands of the attacker. The simple fact is that a given action (the assailant's attack) is faster than a reaction (the countermeasure), which, however swift, will always be at least a split-second behind. Act decisively and block the opponent's efforts immediately to neutralize the attack.

Pagmamasdan mo ang kamay. "Watch the opponent's hands." This principle is a reflection of the fact that the Philippines has traditionally been a weapon-bearing culture. Most violent conflicts involved the use of weapons. While one might also encounter kicking techniques in the arena of all-out combat, attacks in everyday life are most likely to be carried out by unskilled fighters. These assailants will often use a club-type (think lead pipe, heavy stick, or crow bar) or bladed implement (box cutter, short dagger, or folding knife). Keeping an eye on their hands to know what they are carrying and how they manipulate their weapons is vitally important.

Glossary

The modern Filipino alphabet, called *abakada,* consists of twenty letters: a, b, k, d, e, g, h, i, l, m, n, ng, o, p, r, s, t, u, w, y. Vowels are pronounced as such: A as in calm, E as in egg, I as in ski, O as in off, and U as in flu.

Ng counts as one letter and is similar in sound to the "ng" in wing, but appears at the beginning of words such as ngayon (now). The rest of the consonants are pronounced as they are in the English language.

Because accent marks are not used in the contemporary written Filipino language, one must gain a familiarity with proper accentuation in pronouncing a word. The word *daga,* when pronounced with the stress on the first syllable (DAH-ga), means dagger. Pronounced with the stress on the second syllable (dah-GA), and with a guttural sound at the end, it means mouse.

Regional variations in pronunciation often reveal which part of the country a person is from. In some regions of the Philippines, for instance, people will substitute the vowel "e" for "i" and vice versa, and the vowel "o" for "u" and vice versa. Finally, one cannot simply add an "s" at the end of a Filipino word to form a plural. The word *mga* is added before a given word to signify plurality.

abaniko. Fanlike pattern of movement named after the folding fan of Spanish origin.

agimat. A talisman, commonly a stone or religious figure made of metal.

albolaryo. An herbalist. Coined from the Spanish word *herbolario.*

alibata. An alternate term for baybayin.

alipin. A slave. Slaves were one of three social classes in the ancient Philippines.

anting anting. A talisman (same as agimat).

arnis. Filipino fighting art that utilizes stick, blade, and empty-hand components.

aswang. Generic term for "monster" from lower Filipino mythology.

Bahala na. "Come what may," an outlook signifying fatalism, or the surrendering of the outcome of a given conflict to God.

bakbakan. A free-for-all fight without rules.

balisong. A fan knife (also called the butterfly knife in the U.S.) featuring a blade connected by a hinge to two pieces of wood and metal that serve as a sheath.

banda banda. A horizontal pattern of weapon movement.

bara bara. Wild or patternless striking. Early forms of arnis training were often characterized by this description.

barang. A flat-headed long blade.

barangay. A basic community unit.

baston. A walking cane or arnis stick.

bathala. A traditional Filipino term for a supreme being.

bayanihan. Native spirit of cooperation; the act of people working together to move an entire house from one location to another.

baybayin. Ancient Philippine system of writing now in disuse.

bayo. Literally, "to pound." Signifies a blow with bottom of the fist or a pommel blow.

binakoko. A long blade named after the native bakoko fish.

buno. Nondescript form of native wrestling, same as dumog.

cinco teros: Five strikes. Coined from the Spanish term *cinco tiros,* it signifies the old arnis system.

daga. A dagger or fighting knife.

dinahong palay. A long blade named after a poisonous snake.

doblada. A striking pattern that makes an oval shape.

doble baston. A double-stick method of arnis.

doblete. A striking pattern that makes an oval shape; an alternate term for doblada.

dulo dulo. A double-tipped short stick.

dumog. The Visayan term for native wrestling; same as buno.

eskrima. An alternate term for arnis coined from Spanish word *esgrima,* meaning "swordplay."

fraile. An alternate term for arnis coined from the Spanish word for friar.

galing. Skill.

garote. An alternate term for arnis coined from the Spanish term *garrote,* meaning "heavy stick."

guro. The modern-day term for an arnis instructor. It was originally meant to signify a schoolteacher.

hakbang. A step or footwork.

hambalos. To strike with a heavy stick.

hampas. Strike with stick.

hiwa. To slice with a knife.

ilag. Evasion or evasive techniques.

itak. The general utility blade of the Filipino farmer; an alternate for bolo.

kadena. A chain, coined from Spanish word *cadena.*

kalasag. A shield.

kamay. Hand.

kampilan. A long blade from the Islamic south that has dual stabbing points.

Kombatan: The distinct Filipino martial arts system developed by Grandmaster Ernesto Amador Presas Sr.

kris. A wavy or straight bladed sword or knife from the Islamic south.

krus. Cross shape, coined from Spanish word *cruz,* meaning "cross."

krusada. A cross-shape pattern of movement.

kundiman. A type of native dance.

labo labo. Rumble or free-for-all fight, same as bakbakan.

labtik. A snapping strike; alternate term for pilantik.

lakas. Strength.

lakas loob. Inner strength or courage, said to be one of the most vital attributes of an effective arnis fighter.

lamay. Funeral wake.

laslas. To slash or cut to shreds.

Luzon. Main island in the northern region of the Philippines.

mano mano. Empty-hand combat. Coined from the Spanish term *mano a mano* or hand-to-hand.

Mindanao. Group of islands in the southern region of the Philippines.

Moro-Moro. Socio-religious play depicting the triumph of the Christian Spanish over the Muslim Moors at Granada.

ocho ocho. A figure-eight pattern of weapon movement. Coined from the Spanish word *ocho,* meaning eight.

pa-traidor. A sneak attack.

pabayo. Hammer blows delivered with the pommel of the stick.

pagtayo. A stance.

palo. To strike with a stick; same as hampas.

panaksak. Thrusting knife.

patalim. An edged weapon.

pilantik. A snapping strike.

pinayong. An umbrella-like pattern of movement.

pinuti. A white arm, a type of bolo. In the European martial tradition, the term *armas blancas,* or white arms, was a reference to edged weapons (as opposed to *armas de fuego,* or firearms).

pulaw. Funeral wake, same as lamay.

puno. A base or the pommel end of a weapon.

redonda. Double stick twirling.

rompida. An up-and-down pattern of weapon movement.

saksak. To stab or thrust.

salag. To block.

salag tusok. Literally block and thrust; an alternate term for sungkiti.

sangga. To block, the same as salag.

sibat. A spear. It does *not* mean staff.

sikaran. Native Filipino martial art that uses kicks extensively.

sinawali. A method of double stick work that uses a weaving pattern.

sumpit. A blowgun.

sundot. A superficial poke.

sungkiti. An arnis method that emphasizes thrusting techniques.

taga. To chop.

Tagalog. From "taga ilog," meaning "people of the river," Tagalog is a dialect of the northern Philippines that was the basis for the national language called Filipino; there is also a tribe by that name.

tuslok. A thrusting technique; alternate term for sungkiti.

tutsada. A thrusting technique; alternate term for sungkiti.

Visayas. Group of islands in southern-central region of the Philippines.

yantok. An arnis stick.

Recommended Reading List

The works listed below provide a good starting point for martial arts enthusiasts who would like more information about arnis. In addition, readers should check out the excellent Filipino martial arts magazine *Rapid Journal,* which can be accessed online at http://www.rapidjournal.com.

Draeger, Donn F., and Robert W. Smith. *Asian Fighting Arts.* New York: Berkley Publishing Corporation, 1974.

Gagelonia, Pedro. *Philippine History.* Manila: National Book Store, 1974.

Presas, Ernesto A., and Salvador A. Avendanio. *The Art of Arnis.* Manila: Ernesto A. Presas & Associates and Arjuken Karate Association, 1981.

Presas, Ernesto A. *Arnis Presas Style and Balisong.* Manila: Ernesto A. Presas, 1988.

———. *Filipino Armas de Mano Presas Style.* Manila: Ernesto A. Presas, 1996.

———. *Filipino Modern Mano-Mano.* Manila: Ernesto A. Presas, 1996.

———. *Filipino Police Combative Technique.* Manila: Ernesto A. Presas, 1996.

———. *Filipino Knife Fighting Presas Style.* Manila: Ernesto A. Presas, 1998.

———. *Dumog Presas Style.* Manila: Ernesto A. Presas, 2002.

Wiley, Mark, ed. *Arnis: Reflections on the History and Development of the Filipino Martial Arts.* Boston: Tuttle Publishing, 2001.

Zaide, Gregorio F., and Sonia M. Zaide. *History of the Republic of the Philippines.* Manila: National Book Store, 1983.

About the Author

Manila-born José G. Paman is a practitioner, competitor, teacher, researcher, author, lecturer, and perpetual student of the martial arts. He began his journey in the arts in 1971, when he joined the Arjuken Karate Association under Ernesto A. Presas, Sr., studying an early version of Kombatan, as well as Shotokan karate. Two years later, Paman was accepted into the Tong Hong (Eastern Athletic Association) under the leadership of Co Chi Po and started learning the Fukien ngo cho (five ancestor) system of kung fu. He trained at the two gymnasiums concurrently, absorbing a comprehensive knowledge of the arts of arnis, karate, and kung fu. Paman was a member of the University of Santo Tomas Team that won top honors at both the First and Second Intercollegiate Karate and Arnis Tournaments held in Manila in 1975 and 1976.

Paman moved to the United States with his family in the late 1970s and continued to train with practitioners of different martial arts systems. He participated in karate and kickboxing events throughout Northern California and gathered victories in several tournaments, including the Captain Webber Days Karate Championships, the Capital City Karate Championships, and the California State Karate Championships. In 1989 he studied the goshin jitsu method at the Goodwin Dojo under the guidance of Rod Goodwin.

Currently holding advanced black-belt degrees in Ernesto Presas' Kombatan system, Shotokan karate, and goshin jitsu, Paman has served as the Senior Instructor of the Arjuken Martial Arts Club in Sacramento since 1983. He has also co-taught a self-defense class at McClellan Air Force Base in North Highlands, California.

Since penning his first article for a karate magazine in 1987, Paman has written over 100 articles for a number of publications. He wrote the Arjuken Martial Arts Club Basic Training Manual and co-wrote the books *Comprehensive Self-defense* and *Jujitsu Strangles and Strangle Counters* with Rod Goodwin. Paman's works also appeared in the anthologies *The Ultimate Martial Arts Q and A Book* and *The Best of C.F.W. Martial Arts 2000.*